The Path of the Human-Incarnated Angel and Starseed

MARGARET DONER

◖iUniverse®

THE PATH OF THE HUMAN-INCARNATED ANGEL AND STARSEED

iUniverse books may be ordered through booksellers or by contacting:

iUniverse
1663 Liberty Drive
Bloomington, IN 47403
www.iuniverse.com
1-800-Authors (1-800-288-4677)

ISBN: 978-1-5320-4864-7 (sc)
ISBN: 978-1-5320-4865-4 (e)

Print information available on the last page.

iUniverse rev. date: 04/27/2018

Dedication

This book is dedicated to all the human-incarnated angels and Starseeds walking the planet Earth right now. I know it isn't an easy path, but we are not alone. Stay strong, true and fearless.

Note

This book was written prior to the dissolution of net neutrality. As a result, the links I mention throughout the book may not be available after publication in 2018. Currently, (as of the end of December 2017) none of us is exactly sure how the corporate takeover of the internet will impact American's freedom to access information that is not under corporate control. If the links do not work, this is more than likely a result of the FCC decision to end net neutrality.

Contents

PART I   ANGELS AND DEMONS

Chapter 1   The Path Of The Human-Incarnated Angels
And Starseeds 1
Chapter 2   The First Incarnation 30
Chapter 3   Duality Begins 39
Chapter 4   The Teams Form 49
Chapter 5   Other Cultures Speak To Our History 56
Chapter 6   The Family Of Light And The Family Of Dark 64
Chapter 7   The War In Heaven Lands On Earth 77
Chapter 8   Moving Out Of Time 103

PART II   WHAT CAN WE DO?

Chapter 9   What Can We Do? 125
Chapter 10   Protecting Yourself And Releasing
Yourself From Fear 139
Chapter 11   Living The Truth Of You 152

INTRODUCTION

Are You A Human-Incarnated Angel Or Starseed?

Is there a difference between an angel and an Extraterrestrial, or Starseed? You could be an angel, who has never taken on a third-dimensional body, and not be a Starseed or Extraterrestrial. (But that wouldn't apply to anyone reading this, because it would mean you had never taken on a physical body, and clearly you have.)

You can be a Starseed, or Extraterrestrial, and not be incarnated directly from the angelic line. (There are species of Extraterrestrials who are robots, for example.) But, if you are reading this, and you are of angelic origin, you will most likely also be a Starseed. This means that you have been "other" than human, and have incarnated on other planets, and in other dimensions.

Although everything is contained within God/Source energy, not everyone is identical. And, because we have not been schooled in anything beyond this dense plane of existence, we often get very confused when we talk about Extraterrestrial and Extradimensional lifeforms. For example, both ETs, and angels can be *extradimensional*, or EDs, because they often share the appearance of "otherworldliness."

Both ET's and angels are also more advanced than humans,

capable of moving through solid objects and unhindered by time/space. Some Extraterrestrial/Extradimensional beings reportedly glow like angels. Some have power that resembles the ancient gods. Are angels, ETs, EDs, and the gods, the same entities, but titled differently? More and more people are believing that this is so. Our views on angels, and Extraterrestrials, are rapidly changing. If you are interested in this topic, there is a good chance that you are a Starseed, or an angelic being. If you identify with that title, then you will find yourself in good company. There are many more Starseeds, angels, and "otherworldly" beings walking this planet than most people believe. Perhaps you are one of them.

Incarnated angelic beings, and Starseeds, are born with an inherent spiritual awareness that sooner or later leads them to question the false matrix. Since childhood these individuals have known that there is something "not right" about the world around them, and they have challenged the teachings they receive. It's as if they are immune to the mundane, and aware of another reality. Their inherent inner knowing often joins forces with their worldly experience to push them in a direction of greater knowledge. Knowledge brings empowerment, and greater safety, and once the angelic human overcomes their fear of knowing, they step into a powerful place of self-realization and acceptance. Their journey is the mystical and metaphorical journey of "the hero;" the journey to leave home, delve into the depths, and return home once again, but this time with wisdom.

To understand if this is your journey, and your soul's calling, you can begin by asking yourself these questions:

1. Even as a child did you question what people told you?
2. Are you an Empath? Do you tend to take on another person's pain as your own?
3. Do you have the ability to contact people on the "other side?" Are you what people consider psychic?

4. Have you felt the pain of the human race, and worried about the suffering of the world? Do you automatically "think globally," or even "galactically?"

5. Have you had the ability to experience great joy, as well as great pain? Are your emotions intense?

6. Do you just "know things?" Have you often said, "I don't know how I know it, I just do?"

7. Do you live by your intuition?

8. As a child, did you believe you could fly, or have other superhuman abilities? Maybe you still do?

9. Do people call you names such as, "The Angel of Blessings," or "The Angel of Beauty?"

10. Have you been a target for dark energies? Have you been psychically attacked?

11. Have you felt confused when people "attack" you?

12. Have you felt protected and surrounded by unseen energies since childhood?

13. Have you repeatedly said, "I want to go home," and meant heaven?

14. Have you felt that you, "Don't belong here," meaning Earth?

15. Have you found it difficult to close your heart, and found that people take advantage of your open heart?

16. Do you find that other people "don't understand you," and perceive you as odd?

17. Do you feel and perceive the world energetically, and not merely as physical form?

18. Do you believe that miracles are natural, and should be expected?

19. Do you feel personally connected to spiritual beings, and consider them family?

20. Do you love Mother Earth as a "Sister?" Do you feel her pain?

21. Do you question the nature of reality?

If you relate to most of these, it is very possible that you are a human-incarnated angelic energy or Starseed. Perhaps you carry the energy of a great archangel such as Michael, Gabriel, Raphael or Ariel. Or perhaps your energy is that of a cherub. Whatever you are, your journey is shared by others of your nature. You are not alone.

Some of us "human-incarnated angels" remember lives during the time of the historical Jesus. We remember learning from him when he walked the Earth, and we reject the image of Mary Magdalene as lowly prostitute, and instead we relate to Mary Magdalene as Jesus' equal. We see her as his companion and fellow teacher. Many of us rejected the teachings of organized religion in its strict fear-based model and searched instead for a deeper truth and wisdom to guide us. Whether raised outside the Christian religion in this lifetime or not, we often consider Jesus to be a life teacher and guide.

In our past life explorations, some of us have also discovered lives as Essenes, Gnostics, and Cathars, and we have been persecuted for our beliefs again and again.

I contend that what Jesus experienced in his life on Earth, was laid down as a template for those of us in his spiritual school. Those of us who consider him a teacher and friend have followed his teachings through many lifetimes and experienced *in many lifetimes* what *he experienced in the one.* Through our many lifetimes, including this one:

1. We studied metaphysical teachings, Eastern religions and shamanic studies. (This mirrors Jesus' "lost years.")
2. We railed against the "moneylenders," and others who enslave us financially.
3. We met with the Devil and turned down dark contracts and deals that would give us "false power." We chose faith over black magic, fame and power. Having overcome our fear of evil, we learned to cast out demons, as Jesus did. *
4. We suffered as martyrs in many lifetimes. We were burned at the stake, thrown to lions, or stoned to death for our healing abilities. Yet, we maintained our Christed heart.

5. We have been betrayed by our own personal Judas'. We have suffered by trusting those whose envy, arrogance and greed led them to attack us, in the same way that Judas betrayed Jesus.

6. We learned not to, "throw our pearls before swine." The full quote is from Matthew in the bible and it reads, "Do not give what is holy to dogs, and do not throw your pearls before swine, or they will trample them under their feet, and turn and tear you to pieces." This means do not give your gifts away to those who will not appreciate them. How many of us have done this over and over again, only to experience being torn to pieces?

7. We learned that forgiveness of those who harm us is the only path to the ascension of our spirit. "Forgive them, they know not what they do."

Make no mistake, there are Starseeds and angels who could not resist the temptation of dark power. Although, initially, the person feels empowered, the end result is never a good one, because the ego is the guide of this type of practitioner. Their road proves quite difficult, in its own way, but overcoming the darkness can be utilized as another path to the Light.

After having been "beat-up" (or nailed to the cross), we find the teachings of Buddha to help us attain emotional and spiritual neutrality and understand the wisdom of the old soul. We strive to clear the karmic attachments that keep us tied to this lower third-dimensional realm.

Those of you inclined toward the teachings of Carl Jung will see in all of this the "hero's journey," and the figures of Jesus, Buddha, and Judas as archetypes. This is indeed the journey a soul must endure to reach maturity.

I have said that I believe that Earth can be viewed as "boot camp" for the angelic soul. As metaphysical soldiers, we learn to get tough so we can overcome our fear of the dark. Only when we overcome our fear of the dark can we be of use to others. To serve as a guardian angel for other souls, we need to rid ourselves of fear. The only difference between an Ascended Master and an average human is an Ascended Master has met the darkness and overcome his fear of it. We must meet the darkness both within and outside the self if we are to fulfill our true purpose.

Part One

Angels And Demons

CHAPTER ONE

The Path Of The Human-Incarnated Angels And Starseeds

I have been working as a spiritual counselor/past life therapist for over twenty years. I have witnessed changes in the individual consciousness of myself, and my clients, as well as in the collective worldview, over that period of time. I have observed the path of people who felt, since childhood, that they "don't belong here," or that they are different. Most angels and Starseeds want to be awake and aware. But, before we go into a journey to be awake and aware, we should define what it means.

What Does It Mean to Be Awake?

When most people speak of being awake they mean being awake in the physical sense. Overnight I am asleep, in the morning I awaken, that sort of thing. But, awakening as a spiritual being is quite a different idea. Churches proclaim spiritual awakening, and yet, we see much darkness, mind manipulation, and control systems abound in the standardized religions. The New Age movement proclaimed, "spiritual awakening," and yet, as this movement has moved from its infancy, it too, has become tainted with lies and false gurus. (Guru means teacher…and of course, there are both false and honest teachers.) The world is an insane asylum, but, only the awake perceive it to be so. Accepting inequality, poverty, suffering, war and mass murder, as "normal," is insanity. Denying its existence is also a form of insanity. However, humanity is "awake" within that perception. We close our eyes to humanity's suffering and claim to be awake. Are we truly "all one?"

We are *not* born into this reality as a blank state. We carry our other lives upon our "backs," and in our soul's conscious awareness. Angelic beings and Starseeds often access these other lives quite easily. Awakened beings remember that suffering is foreign to the Higher Self, and yet exists everywhere in the lower-dimensional consciousness realms. Being awake means, you feel the vast suffering and the inequality that humanity experiences, and your heart registers it. This is why "being awake" is so difficult for most people, and instead they choose to be "asleep." Many people reject being awake for just that reason: self-protection.

There is a way to be "awake," and not be continually depressed or frightened. It isn't an easy journey, but it can be done. Awakening as an angelic being, or Starseed, is an individual journey. It is truly a journey to Know Thyself. That's why the first step to spiritual awakening is to go inward. Although it sounds simple, it is the hardest thing we can do, and quite often painful. Our egos reject the self-scanning process and continue to urge us to look outside for answers, perpetrators, and enlightenment.

The second step is being honest with what exists around you, and not creating a reality that self-soothes and that masks true reality. Again, sounds simple, but again, a scan of the self will uncover where you change reality to suit your own needs. See people and events as they are, not as you want them to be, and you will be miles ahead in your awakening. A large part of doing this is trusting your instincts, and your feelings. If something isn't right in your world, your gut will tell you. This has never been more important than it is today.

Thirdly, not creating and recreating negative energy patterns for the self. Most people think that is about denying the "bad stuff," so you can "feel good." But, it is far more. It is holding reality in a state of neutrality, while continuing to maintain empathy and emotional responses. It doesn't mean you numb yourself. It doesn't mean you wear a "happy hat," and "drink the Kool-Aid." It means you open your heart in a Bodhisattva manner. If you think that's easy, try it for a week. Examples of a Bodhisattva heart are: Jesus in the leper colonies, Gandhi with the Untouchables, Martin Luther King with the black population in America in the 1960s. They experienced anger, and human emotions, but the ability to put that anger aside to do what they came to do, is reflected in their lives.

Fourth, it is about seeing the "gift, lesson, and blessing," whenever possible. This is not always possible in the immediate. Sometimes it takes many hundreds, or even thousands, of years to tap into that point of view of an event. An example of that is my horrible life in ancient Rome. I was used as a sexual slave as a child (as so many boys were) and emotionally damaged. It wasn't until this lifetime, that I could understand that life in a larger context. Today, I understand and know who my abusers were, and how my innocence has been often used against me. The gift of that past life, is that I choose, in this lifetime, to shed my innocence, and seek wisdom and knowledge. I believe it keeps me safer; and so that horrifying life has led to my desire to seek enlightenment over the course of many lifetimes. That is the gift of the horrors I endured. However, I did not have the ability to integrate that experience in an "awakened" state until this lifetime.

Many Angelic/Starseeds understand this path to healing, and as a result, as a past life regression therapist, and spiritual counselor, I have heard other people's stories of abductions in this life (or other lifetimes) by Reptilian Extraterrestrials, or Gray aliens, or Mantid-Insectoid beings. I have assisted people who have been brave enough to look at their karmic shadow and heal the dark contracts that have held them enslaved for lifetimes. I have also known many who have run away from their own, and the collective shadow, because they were afraid to see the truth of it.

I know that many consider these ideas to be crazy. But, I know that many, many others have walked a similar path, but are afraid to speak of it because they do not have the support they need to speak their truth.

The angelic souls came in particularly innocent, and often they wear the biggest pair of rose-colored glasses a human can muster, and when those get tarnished they simply put another pair on top of them, hoping to continue their rosy worldview, despite the pain and betrayals they suffer. Those who carry the energy of the Angel Grace, or the Angel of Blessing, for example, or appear delicate, and surrounded by fairy or mermaid energies, have the greatest difficulty adjusting to the harsh realities of being incarnated upon the Earth.

Those angelic souls who carry the warrior energy of Archangel Michael, (or other archangels) or the energy of the angels of Courage, Knowledge, or Truth, will find themselves better equipped to handle this planet and the wars that often define it. Because angelic beings are messengers, and they come from a place of unity and peace, they often will find themselves struggling with the lies, deception, secrecy, and powerlessness of being human.

Many angelic/Starseed souls believe they are carrying the energy of an Ascended Master or other large spiritual being. Currently, there are many Mary Magdalenes embodied on Earth who have complete recall of her life on Earth with Jesus, for example. There are also quite a number of people who feel they are the incarnation of Merlin, Artemis, Archangel Michael, Joan of Arc, Lancelot, and so forth. It is important not to ego-attach to these beliefs. First, and foremost, all energy is available to all beings, so no one "owns," any energetic imprint, exclusively. Secondly, these energies are currently being housed in many bodies for good reason. The second coming of Christ was never meant to be in just one body, this second time around. We are all the incarnation of Jesus Christ when we embody his Christed message and heart, and that's the way it is meant to be. There are people who believe they are Jesus on Earth today, but, the energy is not exclusive, and it shouldn't be.

I think the Family of Light must of gotten wise about how to bring these energies onto the Earth to do their work. Spread them around to insure if one dies, or is killed, the energy will still be around, and available. If you find yourself believing you are the only incarnation of an ascended master you will have to watch the state of ego entanglement around this issue. Act as a Bodhisattva and use your energy, and past life recall, to clear karma and any negative energy imprint; be aware that ego attachment will begin to trigger the Reptilian brain. When in doubt, rise above the ego.

I understand that if you believe you are a "famous" or "important" past-life personality there are those who will remind you that this has all the hallmarks of mind control techniques used on people in the well-known MK Ultra experiments. But, transcending the ego-attachment to past life personalities assists even those people. Non-attachment to the information you are receiving and using the information to clear karma, and transcend ego, benefits everyone.

If you are clearing the karma of one of these large energies, such as Joan of Arc, then you might also be an angelic or a Transcendental Soul, who has come back to assist the energy to reunify and heal. These large energy beings, such as Joan of Arc, often need help; and they need more than what one human being can provide, to assist them to heal! If you believe this is you, then this point of view should also be egoless; do your job quietly and with reverence. Others needn't know. If you find it impossible to transcend the ego, then it is more than likely you are adding to the karma, not removing it. If your ego attaches to the information it will be used to drag you down; not lift you up.

It could be said that these famous beings often have very large karma from their time on Earth. In fact, in many ways every dark wizard who has been practicing on the Earth is carrying Merlin's shadow aspect. If you know that you have been a dark wizard, you might realize that clearing your past life karma with dark magic, helps the Merlin energy, upon the Earth, to heal.

Humans create karma, and karma is carried from lifetime to lifetime until it is healed. I explain karma this way: "bad karma" is created when you take away the free will of another human being, in this dimension. It can be big karma, like murder, or it can be smaller karma, like denying another the right to follow their own heart in a career choice. Karma creates energetic cords between individuals; cords that most often hook into the main chakras and draw us toward that individual until the karma is healed. The cords can be created lifetimes ago, or they can even be created during a lifetime off-planet. These cords loosen with only one state of mind... forgiveness. The forgiveness comes, more often than not, from a search through one's past lives. It involves doing a face-to-face with the shadow. Healing takes place through the shadow, for it is the shadow that requires healing.

This book is designed to let those of you who relate to it know that you are not alone. I share these insights and experiences to assist you to find the courage to do the real journey of healing the soul. The journey through the shadow, back into the Light. Light reveals the shadow, shadow hides the Light. Enlightenment will never be achieved through ignoring the shadow or putting on another pair of rose-colored glasses. Strength, truth, courage, and wisdom are all an important part of the soul's growth. These are attained through experience. Do not run from the experiences you have collected through your many lives on this planet, or on other planets, or in other dimensions. These experiences have made you what and who you are. Embrace them as your teachers.

When we hear of billionaires such as Elon Musk (Tesla) and Richard Branson (Virgin) looking to the stars for answers and putting their wealth into dreams of traveling to the moon or Mars, we have to wonder if they too are longing to go "home." Perhaps what they are searching for would be best found within their own souls; and the search outside of themselves to find "home," will never fully satiate their heart's longing.

Below, reproduced from my book: *Merlin's Handbook for Seekers and Starseeds,* is a list designed to assist you to identify various Starseed imprints, and perhaps recognize your own. I thought it was a good idea to restate this information. Some of you may not have read the *Merlin's Handbook,* and others may have forgotten the information. So, below is a refresher. Also, some of the ideas presented later on in the book, are built upon the information listed below. Even if you have read the book *Merlin's Handbook for Seekers and Starseeds,* you might find it helpful to reread the information on Starseed karmic imprints.

Please be aware that many angelic beings will hold <u>more than one</u> of these imprints (as well as other imprints not listed below), as they have been incarnating for thousands and thousands of years.

Essentially, we are galactic immigrants, who escaped other planets, when they were attacked. We came to the Earth in our search for a new home, but, we are not only human. Like Earthly immigrants today, from Syria, Myanmar, or other countries in Africa and Asia we fled our homes when they were destroyed and took up refuge elsewhere. But, we have always longed to return to our "old homes," and we have never felt that we "fit in."

Arcturians: The Arcturians are currently highly evolved spiritual beings who hold consciousness primarily in the fifth and sixth (sometimes seventh) dimensions. During the Orion Wars, unlike many of the other planetary systems, the Arcturians knew that the invaders were coming, and prepared themselves to meet the onslaught by moving out of the third and fourth dimensional lower astral realms, where they knew they would be seen, to higher dimensional realms (fifth and sixth) where they knew they could not be captured. To understand this vibrational shift from the human point of view is to understand that the angels exist alongside us, but in a higher dimensional realm, which we cannot (usually) see or reach. That dimensional barrier keeps them safe from lower dimensional contamination, and this is the same idea with the Arcturians. Although they do not vibrate at the same level as an archangel, they currently vibrate high enough to avoid detection by lower life forms and entities.

When the Arcturians were in danger of being attacked, they protected themselves by enacting this vibrational lift, and those who could not hold the higher consciousness frequencies, and might endanger the majority of the people, were cast-off into space to fend for themselves. Most often the Arcturian was quarantined by a vibrational separation. This means that those who could not sustain a high vibration, and might endanger the entire planet, by lowering its frequency, experienced being alienated.

(Some of you might be reminded of the ideas that were circulated around the Mayan Calendar, December 21, 2012 event. Some believed that the planet would ascend into a fifth dimensional frequency at that time, and those who could not vibrate high enough would be left behind. One could certainly surmise that perhaps this was stimulated by the old memory of the Arcturian experience).

The journey of the Arcturian who did not make the "jump into a higher frequency" is an individual one. There is no one single path that took place after being cast-off, but in the search for a new home many Arcturian souls eventually settled on Earth. Earth is a mish-mosh of galactic beings, and they felt that they would be accepted on this planet. However, like so many Starseeds, human-Arcturians will feel that the Earth is not their true home.

A group of Arcturians did not take human bodies and enter the human soul progression upon leaving Arcturus, and landing on Earth. These are the Gray Aliens that are talked about in various books and movies; the ones with the large eyes and bulging heads. The Arcturians and the Grays look very much alike; but the Gray Aliens are the "unevolved, lower vibrational" expression of the Arcturians. Some of these Grays were captured by the Draconian Reptilians and utilized as a part of their army. Some arrived on Earth, but never took human form. They are creating a hybrid human race which mingles the Arcturian Gray DNA with the human DNA and they are also involved in many of the abductions and subsequent experimentation that has taken place. If you or a loved one has been visited by, or worked with, these individuals you can be certain that you have a karmic tie to them that stems from the Orion Wars. If you are afraid of them it is also important to delve into your past life, galactic karma, so that you can heal those karmic cords.

(This is what Dr. Norma J. Milanovich says about the advanced Arcturians in her book, We the Arcturians. "They are the most loving and non-judgmental beings you can imagine. Their skin is a greenish color. They have very large, almond-shaped eyes. They have only three fingers. They have the ability to move objects with their minds and are totally telepathic. Their source of nourishment is an effervescent liquid that is highly vitalizing to their entire being.")

Please notice this description because it matches the description of the much less friendly Gray aliens. It strengthens my belief that Gray aliens are Arcturians who were captured by Reptilians and their DNA altered to serve the Reptilian agenda.

According to some researchers, Gray, alien-like, bio-robotic beings are being manufactured in deep underground bases in England. To find out more about that you can refer to this YouTube video: *Bases Definitive: Humanity Sleep Walking into the Cyborg Age by Miles Johnston.*

The human-incarnated Arcturian Elders, who enacted the quarantine, and made the decision to separate the Arcturian community by vibration, often carry the karmic guilt of this decision. Prior to the quarantine the community had been very unified, and closed, (by human standards) and the welfare of all Arcturians was the consideration of all others. Now, faced with destruction they had to make a decision to save some of their people or perhaps all would perish. It was a difficult decision for the Elders whose job it was to enact the separation. Some families were ripped apart. Others remember being "lined up" and then sent away.

Those who were "booted off" often repeat the story in their human dramas lifetime after lifetime. They are always searching for a community to belong to, and they often feel unworthy or less than others. Arcturian-humans tend to be asexual, or not very interested in lower vibrational expressions of sex; they may enjoy the closeness it brings but feel perfectly happy to live a life with little, or even no sexual expression. Many Arcturian-humans (especially the Elders) will have lives in monasteries, ashrams, convents and other spiritually-based communities.

Humans who are incarnated Arcturian Elders can appear very aloof and carry the air of being above others. They tend to dislike looking at the shadow side of humanity (and themselves) because it uncomfortably reminds their unconscious of how they pushed away the lower vibrational members of their society. To heal their karma, they must be willing to "get their hands dirty" on Earth by compassionately assisting people to lift their vibration. They must curb their arrogance and tendency toward cold-heartedness, and allow themselves to experience, without judgment, the human emotional range.

Those who connect easily with the Arcturian Motherships are also working with the higher-vibrational Arcturians to heal the ancient karma and give all Arcturians the opportunity to come home again.

The longing for the Arcturian soul often revolves around the need for community, and because of this many Arcturians are attracted to religious and spiritual communities where they can live and worship on Earth; places where they finally feel that they have "come home" and have been accepted. If the Arcturian was "booted off" they can give up their power too easily to someone they consider to be spiritually superior to them. If they are accepted it proves to them that they were worthy after all. If they have put their faith in someone they feel betrays that faith, then they may feel more abandoned than ever, and become embittered or disillusioned.

The lesson is to trust the self and release the need to be accepted by others to feel worthy.

The human-incarnated Arcturian Elders must release their belief that they are superior and be willing to acknowledge the reality around them. They must admit that they are on a planet of duality which contains both good and evil, dark and light, and rather than ignore or rush to "fix" everyone or everything because they know best, they must learn to surrender, and watch, without the need to do something. Earth provides the opportunity to learn from a massive range of experiences and learning to honor many different paths is the task of the Arcturian Elder who has chosen to incarnate upon Earth. To heal the ancient karma, one must first be willing to look at the self and understand where your insecurities lie. The healing involves not pushing away the darkness, and the shadow, but embracing all pieces of the self and others. Truly being non-judgmental.

The Arcturian Motherships exist above the Earth in a fifth and sixth dimensional (and even higher) vibrational field. Those aboard the ships feel some "responsibility" for life on Earth because so many of their people are currently incarnated here. They watch over the Earthlings, and gladly assist when asked. It is especially useful to call on high-vibrational Arcturians for assistance in healing as they are excellent healers.

(The first time I met an Arcturian-human was many years ago, long before I was aware of the various Starseeds. I was at a party and felt compelled to ask a man, "Are you an angel?" He answered, "No, I'm an Arcturian," and then he suggested I read the book, "We the Arcturians").

Pleiadians: The Pleiadians have a very complex soul history. Like their fellow Starseeds from Lyra, some of them left the Pleiades after it was attacked and hid out in the fairy realm on Earth. But, this is not true for all of them by any means, and they can be difficult to categorize. Whereas human-Arcturians will be drawn to spiritual communities which encourage a certain "sameness" among the members, Pleiadian-humans will most often be drawn to lives of artistic expression, beauty, the need to stand-out among their peers with self-expression and individuation. Pleiadians make wonderful artists/singers, dancers, actors, and painters; anything that allows them to express themselves. Because on their "home plane," prior to the invasion, they lived an idyllic existence which gave them the opportunity to "play with energy" and create as they desired, it is common for Pleiadians on Earth to long for a similar type of existence. They are often sensitive, and it is difficult for them to accept the harshness of Earth.

Like Arcturians they may be drawn to spiritual communities, but they will also need to maintain some individual expression and will continue their work as artists and artisans within the community. They often work with crystals to heal and beautify their home environment. Unlike the majority of human-Arcturians, Pleiadians are sensualists and usually will enjoy sex as a creative expression. Pleiadians connect to Mother Earth and they will draw strength from trees, flowers, plants, crystals and animals. They are the classic "tree-huggers."

Some of the Pleiadian planets used individuals who were able to vibrate at a frequency beyond the rest of the society; these beings acted as "Queen Bees" to keep the vibration of their planet high and create a fifth, sixth and seventh dimensional world for the others to enjoy. These beings acted like "towers" and transmitted these frequencies through their bodies. Essentially these beings were angels who joined their energy to protect and maintain the Pleiades.

You might ask, "Why if they vibrated at the fifth, sixth and seventh dimension, were they captured by the lower vibrational Draconians? If the Arcturians escaped by raising their collective vibration to that place, why didn't it work for the Pleiadians?" The answer is that when news of the Orion Wars reached the ears of the Pleiadian "Queen Bees" they began to experience fear, which lowered their vibrational fields. Prior to that point the Pleiades was literally "off the radar" to the Draconian Reptilian invaders. Once again think of how beings such as angels on other dimensions can't be seen by humans because they vibrate too high. Fear, however, lowers the vibration of an energy field, and when the fear began to infect the Pleiadian "Queen Bees," the signals they sent out lowered as well. When the Pleiadians were invaded by the Draconian Reptilians they were either used as slaves, killed, or they were captured, and studied or experimented on, for their abilities. Some were also mated with, and a Pleiadian-Reptilian hybrid was created. The Pleiadian-Reptilian karma is rampant today. For example, many artists with Pleiadian creative energy are "managed" by Reptilian "masters." Many Pleiadians will have Reptilian boyfriends, mothers, fathers and so forth. This is because of the karma that they hold with these individuals; it is their job in this life to step from fear and get their personal power back from these Reptilian-humans.

Pleiadian-humans who remember this invasion report that it was swift and brutal. This fear is repeated by human-Pleiadians today in this manner: they often will say to others, "Don't talk about the dark stuff, or you'll draw it to you." They will run away from people who talk about the "dark stuff" of reality because they fear it will lower their vibration, and they will be attacked by it. If you know someone who does this to you, or if you do this, it is very likely you are dealing with a Pleiadian karmic imprint. Learning to keep your vibration high in the presence of the "dark stuff" is the maturing of the Pleiadian-human soul.

The Pleiadian Queen Bees often want to be responsible for holding up the vibration of a group, but they must learn to "let go" of the ancient task and realize that their job is instead to make everyone their own "Queen Bee vibration." The responsibility for holding one's vibration high is the job of the individual. In other words, each person must "rescue" themselves. Co-dependency breeds weakness, self-responsibility strengthens the individual.

When the Pleiadians were attacked they were like innocent children on a playground who were suddenly invaded by evil. The Pleiadians did not even have a word for evil, or a thought to contain the presence of evil in their midst, and at first, they were merely confused at the sudden appearance of the Reptilian soldiers. They soon discovered that something quite new and awful was happening to them.

The "Queen Bees" were captured and utilized through DNA experimentation and interbreeding. Because they were highly evolved and gifted, the Reptilians did not kill them but kept them as prisoners of war. This karma on Earth has been repeated over and over. Human-Reptilians and human-Pleiadians have been recreating their karma back and forth for many lifetimes. On Earth, when the Pleiadians have expressed their psychic gifts and abilities, they have often been tortured as witches. This has left them fearful, angry, wary or in denial if they are running fast and hard enough from their fear.

Human-Pleiadians are often involved in painful karma with a Reptilian parent, spouse, or even child. If they have become wedded to victim status through many lifetimes, they could be unwilling to free themselves from the bond; if they are ready to be free and take back their personal power, they will struggle to cut the ties that bind. However, upon doing the karmic cord release they will feel lighter, and freer than they have in many lifetimes.

How does a Pleiadian-human heal and become released from fear? First and most importantly for the soul journey is to realize that you are on the Earth to learn to hold your vibration high in midst of lower density. Maturity happens on Earth through overcoming odds, strengthening resolve in the face of struggle, and learning to love with eyes wide open to reality, not by denying it or running away from it. The sooner a Pleiadian-human can strengthen their intention to face fear with bravery, not escapism of any kind, the sooner they will have understood the gifts of being an Earth-human.

(One of my Pleiadian "Queen Bee" clients expressed how she was with money. "Sometimes I feel like I have millions of dollars and imagine myself buying a multi-million-dollar estate, and the next minute I realize I only have $100 in my checking account, and I'm in fear of

poverty! Why is that, and how can I change it?" The angels explained to her that energetically as a Queen Bee she was able to draw and anchor in enormous amounts of Creative God Force; with the help of other Queen Bees, she could supply spiritual energy to the entire planet. When she failed to maintain that, and was cast into fear during the Orion Wars, she went instantly into energetic darkness. The teetering back and forth between being overly-abundant, and poverty-stricken, is the replaying of her old Pleiadian karmic pattern. Money represents creative God-Force energy, and when she feels super-abundant, it suddenly triggers her old wounding, and she falls into the old experience of energetic poverty. To balance this, she must first be aware of it, and then find a mid-way point; notice what amount of money and energy can she hold comfortably, and balance what she receives with what she gives out, energetically).

(Those of you interested in reading books written by a Pleiadian channel might want to begin with the Barbara Marciniak books. Also, Barbara Hand Clow's, The Pleiadian Agenda: A New Cosmology for the Age of Light, is only one of the many books she has published from a Pleiadian perspective).

Sirians (from the Sirius Star System) and the Annunaki: The human-Sirians and the human-Annunaki, just like other Starseeds, have their Orion Wars story. It is important to remember that Earth is currently (at the time of writing this) in the middle of the Orion Wars, even though few humans are aware of this.

Again, all of the karma that has been created throughout the many galaxies has arrived on the Earth for us to heal. No wonder life as a human is challenging and overwhelming! The typical Sirian-human is powerful; but many of them are in hiding. Having misused their power terribly in previous lifetimes, not only do they not admit to others how powerful they are, they often feel overwhelmed by their karma and surprisingly powerless.

The term, Annunaki, in modern times has become a "catch-phrase" for the Sumerian gods, the Illuminati, and the royal Reptilian bloodlines said to rule this planet. The idea of the Annunaki, as presented by Zecharia Sitchin as extraterrestrial beings, has influenced modern thought in this area profoundly. Author of many books, he popularized the information of the planetary body called Nibiru, which he claimed was located beyond Pluto. So, the term Annunaki is open to numerous possibilities for definition. In this book the term Annunaki is utilized to express those extraterrestrial "gods" who came from the Sirius Star System. Some Annunaki do have Reptilian DNA, others may not. The Sirius star system, and Nibiru, contain more than a single life form.

It is my belief that we are just beginning to piece together this complex history, and its impact on humanity. If you think about how little we know about our own Earth history, it makes sense that we are still in infancy when it comes to putting the pieces of our galactic history into the puzzle. As humanity begins to awaken to the understanding that there are millions, billions and even trillions of stars "out there," and we are only one tiny planet in the midst of it all; they awaken to the knowledge that "we are not alone."

Most human-Sirians will be attracted to gemstones and love to wear large pieces of jewelry on their bodies and (if it was a different era) in their hair or in headpieces; but long ago these were not used merely for show. The Sirian-humans understood that these stones carried energy that could be utilized and manipulated to enhance their own power. The elaborate headgear of the Egyptian royalty is a perfect expression of the Sirian soul. Sirian royalty understood how to communicate with extraterrestrials and utilized many different devices to send messages to the Motherships. They also knew how to communicate with beings who dwelt in other dimensions, including the dead. In Egypt only the Starseed royalty were allowed access to the spiritual devices and power structures, and these were carefully guarded, along with the secrets kept in them.

Those of the Sirian-Annunaki lineage are often the wizards written about in books, and as most people know, wizards can be dark or light, but they all hold a great deal of power. The Annunaki

(Sirian royalty) had not forgotten their wizard "tricks" when they landed on Earth, and they continually expressed the powers they had on their home planet. *(During a past life session, one of my clients recalled having the ability to take electricity from the air and direct it through her fingertips. She recalled having the ability to direct the electricity into rock formations that resembled Stonehenge. The ability appeared to "activate" the stone formations. This mirrors the abilities of the PK Man a True Story by Jeffrey Mishlove, PH.D.)*

Tales of Atlantis and the misuse of metaphysical knowledge are directly tied to the Sirian/Annunaki lineage. Most Starseeds will have vivid memories of lives during the time of Atlantis. Many will remember how they, in some manner, either contributed to its fall, or struggled to prevent it. The karma is alive today, as many Starseeds have returned at this time to once again try and stop the self-destruction that hangs over the human race and heal the Atlantean karma.

Because Sirian/Annunaki/humans held a great deal of power, they often suffer karma directly associated with power, and the misuse of power, both physical and metaphysical. Like other Starseeds, it is common for those from Sirius to run away from their karma because it is too painful to recognize. Many Sirians, who held positions of tremendous power in past lives, are actually in hiding, and have masked themselves so that others will not recognize them. Although most humans think that if you have been a pharaoh or king in another life you will be a powerful individual in the modern day, very often this is not the truth.

(The first time, years ago, I worked with such an individual, he came into see me, "unmasked." He had the enormous, elongated skull of the Annunaki and he radiated power that I had not previously experienced. It frightened me at the time to encounter such an individual. I cannot explain it to you; I don't know what happened, but the second time he came to do past life therapy with me, he was "masked," and appeared completely different and looked like a "normal" human.

This Annunaki-human had been a very powerful Egyptian pharaoh in another life. But, in this life was seeking to heal his karmic cords).

Because their karma involves the misuse of power, these individuals will often shy away from powerful lives, and instead attempt to heal their karma in quiet service to mankind. It is important for many of these individuals to reclaim their power and speak up by sharing with humanity the gifts and knowledge they have so long repressed. Once they trust themselves to have authority, without abusing it, many of these individuals will once again take up positions of power. To face their karma, they must be brave enough to step into the shoes of their past life personalities and heal the abuses they created. It is also important for them to recognize that the evolutionary history of humanity is intimately intertwined with them, and that they brought a tremendous amount of information, wisdom and growth to the human race. In other words, it isn't all bad! The libraries and halls of learning are directly linked to the knowledge of the Sirian Starseeds and without them the human race might still be in the Stone Age, or at least in the Bronze Age.

The idea of a round table, where each member of the council holds power, is actually a Sirian creation and comes directly from the manner of ruling there. Each council member would take a position of leadership and it would rotate among the members. The idea of a just and noble rulership as expressed by the Knights of the Round Table heralds directly from the Sirius Star System. Those attracted to the Arthurian energies often have roots in Sirius.

In West Africa the tribe of the Dogon people spoke about a race of people from the Sirius system called the Nommos. They visited Earth thousands of years ago and resembled the mermaids and mermen. These mermaid beings are depicted on temples, and in art of many traditions. Even Isis is sometimes depicted as a mermaid, to link her to the Sirius star system. *(My personal experience has included healing a mermaid who was having serious health issues; when given energetic healing she would immediately return to her mermaid state and enter an altered state of consciousness. I truly believe in the existence of mermaids and mermen. Those who have a link to this mermaid race often connect deeply to the dolphins and whales of today.)*

The Dogons also knew about the triune Sirius star system; they knew that the planet Jupiter has four major moons, and that Saturn has rings, and that the planets orbit the sun. They knew this long before Galileo and the invention of the telescope. They explained that the beings from Sirius told them this information.

The word Annunaki has become corrupted as many people have written about the abuses of these Sirians, but the Annunaki are not merely evil. Like all other Starseeds they have their strengths and their weaknesses. And, like other humans and Starseeds they are evolving here on planet Earth.

(No More Secrets, No More Lies, by Sirian Starseed Patricia Cori, and *El An Ra: The Healing of Orion* a novel by Solara, explore these Orion War ideas.)

Alpha-Centaurians: The Centaurs (half man and half horse) are beings who herald from the Alpha Centauri Star System. On Earth, these are quite often the horse-whisperers and horse lovers. Alpha Centauri is the brightest star in the southern constellation of Centaurus; it is also a binary star system and the closest star system to our solar system. The Centaurs who herald from there were powerful warriors. Of course, anyone can be a powerful warrior should they choose, but Alpha-Centaurians do not fight merely to do battle and feed their blood-lust, they fight for a cause, or to uphold justice, or protect the weak.

During the Orion Wars the Centaurs were defeated, and the species destroyed. The Alpha-Centaurians experienced such total annihilation from the Draconian Reptilians that they carry their personal anger and rage in a very specific way. This was because when they were attacked on their home planet their DNA was disassembled, and the back half of the centaur (the horse), and the front half (the human), were separated by their enemies to weaken them and to "teach them a lesson." That is one of the reasons you don't say to a modern-day Centaur, "I'm going to teach you a lesson," unless you want to get kicked hard. And, they can kick hard! Early on in their human incarnations it is very likely that they fought anything and anyone that opposed them or got in their way. As their soul matures they work for causes without a sword in their hand; but they can be just as fierce.

On Earth a Centaur can be either horse or human. Some have chosen to repeat incarnations as horses and others as human. Much of this can depend on which half they were on their home planet; but not always. If a Centaurian wishes to avoid the difficult human karma, and remain in a horse body for many incarnations, they are certainly allowed to. Many of these horses are the ones who seem more intelligent and sensitive than the "average" horse. When they find their "front half" they bond intensely with their human, and when ridden by that human they will "ride as one." In their heart all Centaurs are looking for their soul mate to complete them (the front or back half), and if the soul mate is still in a horse body they will love them like they would a human soul mate. Often, if they settle for a partner less than a soul-mate, they will be miserable.

Human-Centaurs have to fight desperately against an innate cynicism. They struggle to see the good in the world; they may desperately want to, but it can be a struggle. Their wounding is so deep that they often feel lost and abandoned and can have difficultly meditating or connecting to God. The disconnection feels to them as if their very soul was torn apart, and it is difficult to recover from such destruction. Learning to "love your enemy as yourself," is the spiritual goal of anyone, but an Alpha Centaurian may struggle with this concept more than others. How do you love someone who ripped you, and your entire species, into tiny pieces and made it extinct?

Many of these souls will feel the plight of Earthly animals acutely, and work to protect endangered species. They might work in animal shelters or rescue strays. The Centaurs are *not* wizards. They do not do magical spells to destroy their enemies, as others might.

They do not work in the shadows. They are upfront, and what you see is what you get types. They like their truth spoken plainly and clearly. If they lay a trap it will be in the 3D not in the metaphysical realm.

To heal their karmic wounding the Centaur-human must learn to stand alone and resist the dependency they have on a "soul mate" or "other half" to heal their broken hearts. Learning to complete themselves with direct communication to the Divine will assist them to trust again; they will not feel so wary of others, or alone, because they feel the strength of their inner spirit guiding them.

They need action, not words, to heal. Working for a good cause or helping others will go a long way to making them feel connected to a "family" that holds similar beliefs. Coming to the aid of abused horses or other animals will assist them to feel they are doing some good in the world and remove the helpless feeling that often plagues them.

Lyra and the Fairies: There are Starseeds who do not easily fit into other categories. This is because although they are ancient Lyrian souls, they fled the harshness of the Orion Wars and incarnated for long periods on Earth (and elsewhere) in what is known as the fairy realms. Here they hid out, hoping to find an environment similar to what they left behind. The star system of Lyra gave birth to many creational templates and it was where the cat template was first manifested. There are many, many advanced species throughout the multiverse who are derived from the cat template, and they all worship their Christed being: on Earth known as Aslan. Aslan was depicted as a Christ-Lion figure in the children's book, *The Lion, the Witch and the Wardrobe.* It is important to understand that the perfected "Christ-template" exists for each <u>ensouled</u> species.

Starseeds from Lyra came from a beautiful world of unicorns, rainbows and all the things that cynical humans love to poke fun at. Some of them had the bodies of fairies and could create magical sparkles with the wave of their hands. The evil that invaded, and soon completely claimed their home, was too much to bear, and after searching for a home to land upon (like other Starseeds) they wound up in the closest thing to their old life they could find on Earth: the fairy realm. The Wee People, Leprechauns, Elves, Imps, and Fairies populate the fairy realm and hold open a fifth dimensional world both above ground and also inside the Earth in an inner world dubbed Agartha. The struggle for a human-fairy, and human-elf, is to hold truth without running away when they feel threatened by the third-dimensional darkness. Coming into soul maturity for an ancient Lyrian is challenging; the longer spent in the fairy realm the more challenging the integration. Because they often choose to flee rather than fight, their inner warrior is sometimes under developed. They will have to learn how to defend themselves, and reclaim their power by standing to fight, rather than fold, when appropriate.

Human-Lyrians, fairies and elves will naturally be drawn to all things of the nature realm, such as aromatherapy, crystals, and herbs, and will often be involved with stabilizing and re-gridding the Earth to maintain balance in the face of dark forces who challenge their fifth dimensional realms. Because their systems can be delicate, they need to constantly monitor their physical bodies and make sure they do not put too much strain on them. They are often prone to allergies, and chemical insensitivity. Finding the balance between the dualistic Earth energies of good and evil can be very taxing on these humans, and it is important for their survival that they learn to take care of themselves emotionally and physically.

Andromeda: Like many other Starseeds, those who herald from Andromeda have a complex soul history. Much of it depends on the individual's story. Many Andromedans will resonate with sacred geometry and mathematical formulas, understanding almost intuitively how these building blocks are a part of the sacred nature of all creation. This knowledge was particularly useful to the Draconian army, and so when they enslaved the Andromeda planets to acquire the knowledge they did not destroy, they dominated. Human-Andromedans tend to fall into two categories: those who loath technology, due to their karmic role in the destruction it has caused throughout the galaxies, or those who are fascinated with technology because of their role.

It is important to state here how the Andromedan scientists were used by the Draconians to create a robot race, spaceships that could move through time and space, create the cloaking and veiling devices, and the splicing of DNA between species. (It is not my, nor Merlin's, intention to repeat all the information contained in my previous book, *Merlin's War*, however, some of that information must be repeated here). Many of these scientists are alive on the Earth today and their karma is quite evident in the scientific evolution of the Earth, both in positive and negative ways. Nikola Tesla and Albert Einstein, both of whom had tremendous knowledge of metaphysical and physical principles, have had their inventions and mathematical formulas used for both positive and negative outcomes. As the Sirian Starseeds carry a great deal of Atlantean karma, so too do the Andromedans. The brilliance of the technologies, such as running transportation along the ley lines of the Earth to power the vehicles, are typical of the inventions of the Andromedan-humans. These inventions can be seen, both destructive and creative, in the modern world, as well. Scientific inventions are being used to both enslave and free mankind, and depending on how the inventions are applied, and into whose hands they fall, will determine which impact they have.

The Andromedan scientists have an important karmic role to play, but what gives them their brilliance, often blinds them to deeper awareness. The less brilliant among them won't believe in anything they can't touch, or at least prove with a formula, and refuse to open their minds to see what is often right in front of their faces. They are also deeply susceptible to arrogance, and when this occurs they can be insufferable. The Andromedans with this karmic imprint will benefit by humbling themselves to accept that they are not masters of all they survey, and that they have much to learn. Their resistance comes from the unwillingness to revisit painful past-life karma from a time when their inventions were the cause of suffering for so many.

On the other end of the spectrum are the whistleblowers. Those who attempt to heal their karma by exposing the misdeeds of others. Those who have worked in military, and other organizations that abuse power, and then decide to expose the injustice they discover there, are often working with Andromeda karma. Unfortunately, they often pay the ultimate price for standing up for their principles. They pay with their lives, or freedom.

(I worked with an Andromedan-human who discovered that she punished herself for many lifetimes due to her karmic complex. While in Andromeda her inventions had been used to harm others: On Earth we might compare this to Einstein, a seemingly peaceful man whose brilliant concepts brought about the atomic bomb, which was used to kill millions. My client was abused and enslaved lifetime-after-lifetime due to the karmic complex she carried, which created a belief in her that she deserved to be punished. Through this I also came to understand how the Dark Forces will often target these individuals, making sure they don't reawaken their brilliant gifts, because otherwise, they could free people on Earth from the very devices they had helped to create).

Wealthy individuals, and governments often control these individuals (because they have the money to support the research), and it is easy for their inventions to have dire consequences. It is important to note, for example, that many of the scientists involved in the development of the atomic bomb, or the space program, such as Werner von Braun, worked first for Nazi Germany before working for the US government. For many years after WWII, Von Braun worked with the U.S. Army in the development of ballistic missiles. As part of the military operation called "Project Paperclip," he and other Nazi scientists were brought to the United States. They worked on rockets for the U.S. Army, and became the precursors to the United States space program. The sides are always blurred for the Andromedan scientific mind.

The tendency, because they are so brilliant, is for them to believe that they are worldly and not naïve. But, in fact quite the opposite is often true; because so many of them can "talk over the heads" of average humans, the assumption is that they are smarter in all things. But, they are easily tricked because they do not always have fined-tuned sensibilities about human motivation and behavior. Aka: street-smarts. Quite often they aren't interested in humans; they are interested in their work. They may think they know who is good and bad, but in truth their people skills in these areas are sorely lacking. Those of you familiar with the television show, *The Big Bang Theory,* will recognize *Sheldon Cooper* as a broadly-sketched Andromedan character. Growth occurs when the Andromedan-human scientist admits their limitations and puts heart and conscience before mind.

Reptilians and Reptilian-humans: All humans have a "Reptilian brain." Also called the Triune Brain, it is said to be responsible for our more basic, "less evolved," impulses. Growing out of the Reptilian aspect of the self is essential to evolution, and an argument could be made that the baser emotions ruling human behavior, such as jealousy and greed, are a direct result of the lower brain and Reptilian functions. So, some might argue that all humans have some Reptilian in them.

Some, however, believe this is a result of direct DNA tinkering by the Reptilian Race when they first arrived on this planet, long ago. Some believe that they genetically altered the human race by also unplugging our DNA from twelve to two strands. This was only one of the ways they have kept humans "down," and "asleep." It is well known that the human race has been functioning with only a small percentage of their brain power being used.

(The author, David Icke, and his book *The Children of the Matrix: How an Interdimensional Race has controlled the World for Thousands of Years-and still does,* documents his beliefs in this area). According to this theory, there are humans who are more Reptilian than human. These beings, and their ability to "shape-shift" between human and "demon," is well-documented by many cultures and individuals worldwide. These demonic beings "hide" in, or possess, human bodies. When we see them shapeshift, they have either densified into a third dimensional vibrational field, or we have opened our "psychic sight," to the lower fourth dimensional astral plane they are hiding within. Remember our vision is limited to a lower density vibrational frequency field, but it doesn't mean that everything exists within our perceptional abilities. We can only perceive a limited light range. Their appearing to shapeshift is actually a vibrational shift on their part, or our part!

(I have witnessed a human being do this type of shape-shift right before my eyes; I was terrified, of course, at the time. But, I now understand what I witnessed. I believe I was "given" this event so that I could relay this information with the knowledge that it was, in fact, real. I also have sympathy with those who have trouble believing this is true; I wouldn't believe it either, if I hadn't seen it myself).

The Draconian Reptilians (from the Draco star system) are responsible for the origination of the Orion inter-galactic wars and their influence on Earth appears to be widespread. This information is just beginning to be understood by Earth humans. Most people continue to doubt it, for if they have not had direct experience with a Reptilian being, it is not a part of their reality. Fortunately, the combination of people "waking up" to past life and galactic memories, and people speaking up about their present life interactions with these beings without fear, is spreading knowledge of their existence.

If you can accept a lower ET, or interdimensional form of entity, then you might be able to accept that they are responsible for the Lower Matrix of Control that rules much of the darkness on this planet. There are those who believe that this matrix of control originates off of this planet, elsewhere in our solar system. (Saturn and the moon). It appears that the genetic tinkering did not end with the ancient human/Reptilian hybrids but continues today through the work of human-Reptilian scientists.

Most people believe that a soul cannot be snatched; I believe that this is incorrect. At the time of death, or under intense torture to a point close to death, the soul abandons the body. The soul is an electromagnetic field of energy which can be "captured" and held. The Reptilians learned, over many hundreds of thousands of years, and much experimentation, how to capture a soul and reprogram it. It can then be reinserted into the original body, or into a clone. Through implantation, much like a computer, the clone becomes under the control of the Handler. The soul has been reprogrammed. There are those whose souls appear "dead," and unable to express human emotions such as compassion. Perhaps it is worth another look, at why this may be true. Perhaps the soul has been compromised; or perhaps the soul is Reptilian of origin and not human.

Simultaneously, there are also humans who made contracts with the Draconians while undergoing intense torture in an "off-planet" experience. These individuals under duress of torture agreed to work with the Reptilians. If your journey to off-planet experiences brings up such a memory then you were such an individual and still carry the implant today. What is important to realize is that the contract to carry this device is under your free will to break; however, many of the individuals who carry this contact believe that they cannot break it, or do not desire to do so. It is very possible that the implantation and enslavement has been going on so long that it has become comfortable. The fear of breaking the contract is too intense.

Not all ET implants appear to be Reptilian in nature. It seems that many may be placed to track and study human beings. I have met a number of Pleiadians, for example, who believe their implants are benign. Perhaps these were placed much in the same way we tag an animal, to track their movements and study their behavior. Are these implants being utilized to understand the human race better? Are those who agree to carry them assisting their ET friends to study and understand the human race? The implants which control human behavior and create violent reactions in their subjects are clearly of Reptilian or Reptilian-human origin. Those which appear more benign may not control the owner of the implant but track them instead. The question you must ask yourself is: "Am I allowing this of my free will?" In my opinion, all implants should be removed.

(I recently energetically disarmed an implant in my client's right temple that had been put there by the Praying Mantis ETs, and my client's severe back pain immediately cleared up. I have also heard of a number of people having actual non-human, metallic, implants removed by surgeons.)

What about all the cloning that is going on today, and the talk of "self-aware" robots that we are creating? Is it true that if the being is "soulless" they engender no karma? It appears this is so. Karma is a soul-contract; no soul, no contract. Once the soul is reconnected to the Light-Source, karma is re-attached. Avoiding karma is a major intention of the Dark Forces, and they have learned a number of interesting ways to circumvent it. The creation of these robotic beings is one sure way; no soul, no conscious, no karma. Just like a computer is karma-free, so too is a robotic being.

Many "psychics" have been implanted, and are under the control of Reptilian Handlers, and they can be either aware, or unaware, that their power is not coming from the Light, but from the Dark. (Ted Owens, the PK MAN, claims to have been working with Space Intelligence in his abilities, for example.) Sometimes a psychic may have been in the contract for so long they can no longer recognize it. They do not know the difference between receiving information from the Dark and the Light. The simplest way to tell where the information is coming from is to ask yourself, "Do I experience liberation from direct spiritual "knowing?" A higher knowing is liberating and frees you; because of this you will know your knowledge is in alignment with your Highest Truth. It is not a "voice in your head" telling you what to think or do.

Being heart-centered in your approach to life is the clearest way to avoid the dark agenda. The Reptilian implanted self is ego-based, and knowledge is not used to liberate, and enlighten, but to enslave. Dark witches and warlocks are often implanted and although they appear to be "all-powerful" and their clients marvel at how much information they have about the client's life; much of it is being downloaded from a Draconian source.

It appears, through various reports, that Reptilians who have not been blended with human DNA can easily move between dimensions. Sometimes they will appear as "ghostly" visitors in the bedroom, or underground in caves. Both modern and ancient shamans talk of their encounters with these beings. They are fierce and powerful warriors.

Spider Race - I know little about them personally, and yet I have encountered stories about them repeatedly from my past life therapy clients. At one time these beings appear to have been able to conquer other worlds and did so quite extensively throughout the universe. Highly parasitic in their approach, they would completely overwhelm a planet and use the captives for food. (The rampant spider phobias on Earth today come from these earlier experiences of being captured, bound and eaten.) The galactic spiders are enormous and quite clever however, they were not as technologically advanced as other species and reportedly the race was profoundly weakened when their home base, and many other systems they had conquered, were eradicated by Andromedan teams of scientists. These scientists apparently developed the ability to destroy the actual suns that fed the Spider Race planets. Difficult for humans to imagine I suppose. But, reportedly it is then that the Spiders realized they had better become technologically savvy to survive. Over the next hundreds of thousands of years, they joined with the Draconian Reptilians to assist in weaving and maintaining the prison Matrix around a captured planet. I believe they were depicted as the Sentinels in the *Matrix* movie series.

CHAPTER TWO

The First Incarnation

At some point, if a client works with me long enough, I will assist them to return to the state of consciousness they had when they were still a part of The Oneness. This is the time of consciousness prior to the establishment of an individual ego; this is the time when a soul attains enough consciousness to experience the nature of a separate reality, yet not enough to feel alone. In this state of being, a soul feels completely held within the loving womb of God. There is no fear, because the soul has yet to experience separation. There is no feeling of being alone, because the soul has never been alone.

Held in a loving embrace for eons, pure consciousness enjoys this joyful state of simple, loving expression. (Yes, it mimics the womb experience for a human fetus, however, the human fetus can experience pain, both emotional and physical. A fetus, being conceived within the body of a heroin addict, in the midst of emotional turmoil and violence, registers these experiences. These first souls do not, ever, experience pain.)

Every person has a story to tell about how they first separated from the One. Not only do the "hows" differ, so do the "whys." Curiosity is one of the more common reports of venturing out from God. Eons of time (I know there is no time in that state of consciousness, but it is a commonly accepted way of expressing the concept) being held in the womb of God is all well and good, but as the soul "ages" it begins to sense something outside of its own world. Some of the reports from the "curious" souls are: "I wanted to see what was over there," or "my innocence led to my curiosity, like a toddler is curious." These people report seeing something happening, something quite outside of their normal experience. They sense a dark mass or form in the distance and want to check it out. Or they begin to notice "others," and want to explore the energies they are "picking up." These people report that they wandered innocently into dangerous territory. Because they did not have the knowledge to protect themselves, they ventured into perilous situations. Recently, one of my clients felt she was pulled toward the "dark side" from the very beginning; she said she didn't have enough power to resist the original pull.

Another common theme is a feeling of being thrust out into the darkness and fear. There appears little time between an individual's consciousness registering an external energy and the experience of fear. These people are often highly intuitive, and they begin to sense something "different." They might report, "something isn't right," or "this energy doesn't feel good." They often report being captured quickly by dark beings, non-human entities. They feel lost and they report thinking, "why am I being punished?" or "what did I do wrong?" or even, "why is God punishing me?"

Those of you who are reading this may recognize yourself in the experiences of others. Perhaps you have said these things yourself.

The third most common theme is adventure. These souls appear to have a strong separation and ego push, that sends them out from the Source. They too are innocent, but excited to try a new experience. They want to "know it all," and experience it all. They are the brave explorers and often have a fearlessness that pushes them into new situations.

Whichever way a soul chooses to seek moving out from Oneness, that first experience shapes the individual's consciousness throughout its many incarnations, both human and non-human. A *Samskara*, or mental/emotional complex, is laid down that continues to create, over and over, throughout many incarnations, and it defines much of what an individual understands to be true about the nature of reality. Consciousness creates, and recreates, such beliefs as, "I am unworthy," "God abandoned me," "It's not safe to venture out." A person might also hold a great deal of anger at God for creating evil and wonder why. Some people feel tainted by their journey into evil and darkness. Few individuals see themselves as the mythological character known as the Prodigal Son, returning home at the end of their journey through darkness, pain and fear, with new knowledge, wisdom, and a greater appreciation for the "Father's" love.

As I define it, the Earth realm, that we are all familiar with, consists of the Lower Astral, third and fourth dimensional states of consciousness. Third dimension is defined by what we can see, touch, taste and smell...limited by our five senses. Fourth dimension is the lower astral energy that connects to the third dimension and impacts us in an unseen manner. Those with a sixth sense understand this world intuitively; but, make no mistake, it impacts all of us.

For those of you who define the lower astral realm as only the third dimension, in my opinion, it is a matter of semantics. To me, the fourth dimension still contains duality, and the fifth does not. But, these are merely words. Dimensional states of consciousness are what we "title" them to be. I choose to title the lower astral "unseen" realm as the fourth dimension. Thus, the lower astral realm, to me, is the third and fourth dimension. I was taught this, and it makes sense to me. I will use this definition throughout the book, however, please feel free to define dimensional reality as you choose. I have no problem with you using *your* definition of lower astral realm, as you read this book.

We have all heard the idea that our consciousness creates our reality, but, this idea is rarely demonstrated to our satisfaction while in our physical vessel. Human earth life is very dense. However, our soul, unencumbered by the dense physical vessel, creates reality instantly. Our soul, and our consciousness, are essentially the same thing. When we cast off the "mortal coil" (as Shakespeare put it) we become something much lighter…we become the pure energetic expression of our human selves. We become our soul…we become pure consciousness.

Every person experiences a different death. And, every death is different each lifetime. The reason for this is that your consciousness creates reality upon death. You aren't going to see Jesus after death 4000 years ago, because he wasn't in your consciousness, and a death which is peaceful will create a different passage than a death during war.

Energy left behind in the lower astral plane (fourth dimension) contains the consciousness "left behind." This is consciousness too dense to rise above this realm. Ghosts are said to inhabit the fourth dimension, and the more energy left behind by the departing soul, the more likely he (or she) is to be a ghost. You can be alive right now and have a ghost of you stalking a Civil War battlefield. Indeed, your consciousness fragments are strewn throughout the fourth dimensional realm until you recollect and reintegrate them.

My more than twenty years of experience, taking people through their deaths in other lives, shows me that sometimes a soul returns to the Earth quickly, without processing the life just left. Other times a soul rises above the lower astral realm and does a life review. A person who processes the life left behind, before re-selecting another body, evolves much more quickly. Instead of reacting to an unhealed event in the life just past, and choosing revenge for a perceived injustice, a more evolved soul will let go of the anger or fear, leave it behind in the lower astral realm, and raise themselves above the emotional cord that drags them back into density.

To leave behind the karmic wheel of reincarnation forever, a human being must clear up the emotional cords of density that continually drag him/her back into a physical vessel. When the emotional/mental/physical karmic ties are released, the individual continues the journey "home." Now, however, the soul learns in the higher planes of existence. A Bodhisattva is a transcendental soul who vows to continue reincarnating into a physical vessel, to help other humans to release their karma and ascend. Every Bodhisattva knows that each time they return to Earth they run the risk of being "re-hooked" into the lower density of the third dimension, and trapped into the wheel of reincarnation once again, until their karma is cleared.

How does all of this relate to the first incarnation? It appears that although the soul's consciousness gains wisdom and knowledge through its many incarnations throughout time/space, the original wounding follows us. Whether we feel abandoned by God, angry at God for creating evil, punished by God and deserving of the suffering, or evil ourselves, once we are tainted by darkness, we recreate this original wound and add to it, lifetime, after lifetime. The more we "know ourselves" the more we begin to recognize that our original wound has been dogging us for a long time. A very long time.

The longer we carry this wound the more complex the karma (often built around this original emotional complex) becomes. In the younger soul ages (infant, baby and young) we are like children thrashing out, acting out, without the wisdom to understand that we are creating our own hell. As the soul matures (in the mature and old soul ages) the human gains the ability to self-reflect. In the end, the human realizes they must self-redeem. They realize that the Kingdom of God is within them, and that redemption comes from a journey taken within, to Know Thyself, not by putting energy into others and asking them to redeem you. Trusting your inner knowing is a sure sign that you are growing up in soul age.

Connected to our lower consciousness is the need to rescue and save others. We play a game of perpetrator/victim and we look toward others to save us. The biggest victims will always become the biggest perpetrators. Unable to take personal responsibility for their karma and recognize that their own words and actions recreate their personal hell, these people turn everyone into their perpetrator. If you try to save one of these people, eventually you will become their perpetrator. It is easier to blame others than to look in the mirror. Energy vampires will suck you dry, and then turn on you when you refuse to continue feeding them. They often create emotional/mental ditches so deep that they can't find any way out other than to continue the old patterns.

We have all played the game of reincarnation, and because of this we will experience many different states of being: Male/female, rich/poor, victim/perpetrator, powerful/powerless, judge/judged. The first incarnations often hook a soul into creating more female, or male lives, for example. The Samskara (mental/emotional complex) will lay down a belief that, "men are bullies," and create more female lives; or "women are helpless," and create more male lives. But, every soul has the potential to create either male or female lives. Being born into the body of a woman, but wanting to be a man, (or vice versa) as so many are expressing these days, is the soul indicating discomfort due to suddenly being housed in an unfamiliar vessel. Sometimes, however, the Higher Self wants to challenge the human being to try a different sexual expression. Sex changes allow the human ego to say, "Nope, don't like this," even after incarnating.

Until we become more aware of ourselves in the bigger picture, our world will continue to be a reactive Young and Baby Soul playground. Young and Baby Souls often desire positions of power, and they look to others to save them. This is because they are like toddlers, exploring the world outside of them. They lack the inner wisdom of the Older Soul; they do not have enough inner wisdom, or collective knowledge born from experience, to turn inward to find God. Mature and Older Souls often feel trapped in a Baby Soul playground. That is why so many of them long to return to a more peaceful and kinder world, and why they often feel they are talking to a room of toddlers. Each soul age is limited by their experiences.

It is your job to figure out your own soul age and the lessons you came here to learn. (In my book: *Merlin's Handbook for Seekers and Starseeds*, I detail some of the indicators of each soul age.) It's also your job to understand the karma you came here to heal. You can't move to the Transcendental Soul age until your karma is neutralized. Your personal triggers are keys to your unhealed self. That is why a Bodhisattva will always say, "Thank you," when they are verbally attacked. They see the attacker as their biggest teacher. If they react to the attack they know that they are being gifted by the realization that they have some personal emotional healing to do. They know they gave their power away to another. If they feel neutral to the attack they know they are exactly where they need to be.

The quicker our Bodhisattva or Higher Selves become our main avenue of consciousness, the quicker we learn to see the world as our teacher, and the less likely we are to see others as our enemy.

Because angels do not have ears, (they are, after all, not third-dimensional beings, and they do not have bodies) they communicate telepathically. They reside above the lower astral plane of existence. Angels do not need you to "talk out loud," and they are never too busy to assist. However, they do pick and choose, at times, who to attend to. They don't answer every call if it doesn't serve your higher purpose. They are not in the "wish granting" business. They reside above the genies and the Djinn. The genies and Djinn (Middle Eastern word for demon) will trick humans and manipulate humans and could care less whether the wish they grant you serves your higher purpose. Angels care very much about your higher purpose. Sincerity, and a desire to serve a purpose higher than the ego's purpose, will guarantee a "good" angel will answer the call. If you have a lesson to learn, they might not intervene. They won't erase your karma, but they will help you to understand your karma. The "good" angels vibrate much higher than the average human's ego.

Many people are confused by how much they should act in the face of a perceived evil. They believe that if they ignore evil it won't get power over them. This has not proven to be true. Evil exists, and its job is to insert itself into good. Human life teaches through moral choices; you are as you act. It allows us to know ourselves with harsh clarity. Times of great evil allow us to know ourselves with even greater clarity. Do you turn in your Jewish neighbors to save your own skin during your lifetime in Nazi Germany? Do you realize that the soul is worth saving, and that the soul is defined by the choices made?

The third dimension requires action…and defines the soul's current consciousness with a harshness that most people find difficult to address. It is said that if you can act upon your highest consciousness in this lowest density plane of existence, you can probably act upon it in any dimension. Whether that is true, or not, the idea it expresses *feels* true. Expressing the Highest Aspect of our consciousness, while being incarnated in a very dense and violent world, is certainly a challenge. The Earth provides a very intense place for the soul to learn lessons and grow. Seeing ourselves clearly on Earth, means looking into our original wounding, and addressing the shadow self.

While you are alive on the Earth, housed in a third-dimensional body, you are also alive in many other dimensions, simultaneously. This is most clearly demonstrated by the fact that you can access your Higher Self, or God Consciousness, which sits in a much higher dimension of consciousness than the third, while alive in this dimension.

Try this exercise. Sit quietly, breath, and calm the mind and body. Balance your chakras with the colors, red (root), orange (abdomen - second chakra), yellow (solar plexus -third chakra), green (heart – fourth chakra), blue (throat – fifth chakra), indigo (third eye chakra), violet (crown - seventh chakra), and white (eighth chakra about a foot above the head.) Just imagine these colors as a ball of light in each location. It's not difficult. Use your imagination to see each ball of light. Once you feel at peace, and in harmony, lift your consciousness to heaven by imagining yourself "sitting" with the angels and ascended masters. Call on your Higher Self to be visible and visualize what it looks like.

Ask your Higher Self for advice on a current issue or problem. Listen. Dialogue with your Higher Self.

With this exercise, you have just managed to be in two dimensions at the same time. You bridged heaven and earth.

Accessing your past life selves is just as simple, once you know how. First access your Higher Self, and then ask your Higher Self to show you a past life image that will help you to understand your current dilemma. Follow the image you are shown, as you dialogue with your Higher Self about it. You will have a much deeper and more profound understanding of your current life when you learn to do this exercise.

You are alive in many dimensions and many points of time, and there is a Higher Self angel, that is you, in heaven, and a third-dimensional angel, that is you, on Earth.

CHAPTER THREE

Duality Begins

Duality begins with the separation out of the One. It is said that in order for God to know Himself, He had to create consciousness that served as a mirror of reflection back at the Self. (Please note that I will refer to God as He, but I do not believe God is He. I believe God is, in fact, the energy that creates life within all beings, and is much larger than a single pronoun.)

It is said that one of the worst forms of torture a human being can endure is isolation for long periods of time. A person will go insane without the reflection of another being; if a human isn't available, a mouse, bird or even a volleyball, as in the Tom Hanks 2000 movie, *Cast Away* will be created as a substitute. If these are not available, the person will hallucinate friends. If man is made in God's image, then certainly God would create outside of the Self to better understand the nature of reality. Creation sprang from the One in order for consciousness to exist.

If being held in the womb of God feels like bliss, then the illusion of being separated from God feels like the proverbial "being kicked out of the Garden of Eden." Although, as enlightened teachers are quick to point out, we are never really separate from God, and are always contained within God's body, or energy field, it feels like separation to the individualized soul. The individualized soul looks back at God and feels that a separation has occurred. As painful as this is to the soul, (and the karmic complexes grow from this belief) God enjoys the ability to Know Himself through the actions of His creations. Since a piece of Him remains intact within each ensouled creature, He is always with you as long as the soul is intact.

The soul gives you access to your Higher Self, and this is the reason why spiritual teachers will often say, "Your ego may hate what's happening to you, but your Higher Self is learning and growing through the experience, and so quite enjoys it." Your Higher Self is your God Self and sees creation with distance and greater neutrality. Much like good parenting requires the mother and father to "let go," so their child can learn, so does your Higher Self give you free will to experience and create.

Angelic energies have signatures that house huge vibrational frequencies, and their consciousness is big enough to span the universe. They vibrate "close to God" because they are the first-born children. They are indeed the Ancient Ones, and if you look at the family tree from enough distance you might realize that all beings spring from the Ancient Ones. Millions of years later the tree is quite big, but the tree is still All One family. All *ensouled* beings contain a soul, which is a particle of God-Source consciousness. The energy of God is contained within the Angelic Energies, or as they are known in other cultures: The Gods. The largest angelic energy is known (to the Western World) as Archangel Michael-Lucifer; or Michael the Lightbearer. Lucifer means Bearer of Light, and it is Michael's split into two separate energies, Michael and Lucifer, that began the true nature of duality as we know it. Although most people put archangels in a class lower than the Seraphim, Michael is not to be thought of in this manner. Perhaps it is best to think of Michael and Lucifer as angels who "Arch Over" other beings.

Once energy beings separated from God, they had the ability not *only* to look back upon God, but to look at one another. This gave them the ability to see how they are alike, and to see how they are different from one another. Like siblings they loved each other deeply, and like siblings, they began to spat. Lucifer was known as the Lightbearer, and he saw himself as an enormous energy…and, he believed that he was the most important created being out of the One, and a reflection of God Himself. He looked at Michael as his inferior. Certainly, thought Lucifer, he was the closest to God than any separated entity could possibly be.

Lucifer looked at Michael and didn't like what he saw, and Michael looked at Lucifer and didn't like what he saw. He saw Lucifer as arrogant, selfish, and with the intention to usurp all power. Lucifer looked at Michael and saw his limitations, and this made Lucifer uncomfortable. Lucifer began to ponder the idea that if he and Michael are brothers, and if Michael is limited, then he too must be limited. (Hence, Archangel Michael became Lucifer's shadow and Lucifer became Michael's shadow.)

The idea that Lucifer was equal to Michael became impossible for Lucifer to hold, as he believed he was in all ways superior to his brother. He believed he shone more brightly, and his name reflected that fact. Michael was obviously below him in stature, and the more Lucifer looked at Michael, the more he hated what he saw. The more Michael looked at Lucifer he felt something very new to his consciousness; he felt mistrust. Over thousands of years the brothers grew further and further apart, and as they grew further apart, duality grew.

In the meantime, others were created. Angelic beings with different and individual energy signatures had begun to push their way out of the womb: Seraphim, Cherubim, Thrones, Dominions, Virtues, Powers, Principalities, Archangels and Angels. Each of these sprang directly from God Source and each one had an enormous energetic signature. Humans cannot conceive of the enormous consciousness, or abilities of these beings. Angelic beings are defined essentially by their energetic signatures, and they fit into the category based on their abilities. Their abilities are determined by their vibrational signature.

Most people are told that all beings spring directly from

God, and it is true that all *ensouled* beings have within them a concentrated particle of God. We call this concentrated particle the soul. It is, however, the angelic beings alone who span worlds. When incarnated in a human vessel, humans do not span worlds; humans are limited by their five senses (or sometimes a sixth) and operate in the lower astral realms. They are stuck in a vessel that holds them tightly to the lower worlds. Angel vessels are essentially unlimited, and they span dimensions, they span worlds. This is why many people can simultaneously carry the signature of one great angel; Michael for example. His energy must be spread throughout a number of human vessels, because one human vessel could not contain all of Archangel Michael. The human vessel is quite limited, an angelic vessel is basically unlimited.

When a human being dies, they do not become an angel, per se. For humans are (for the most part) still tied to the wheel of reincarnation that keeps them in the fourth and fifth dimension upon death. Angelic beings live in much higher dimensions than humans. Many people believe that their dead relative is their angel. Yes, a dead relative can be a spiritual guide to them, but a human doesn't automatically become an angel upon death.

The original war is the war between the angels. Just like on Earth, teams started to form. Some fell in behind Lucifer, feeling that he was the more powerful of the two, and deserved to rule heaven. Others fell in behind Michael, sensing that Lucifer was becoming dangerously arrogant. If indeed the old adage, "As above, so below," is accurate, we can recognize our own divisions on Earth in the same manner.

Angels, it is said, have no free will. I beg to differ. Although their proximity to the Source makes it appear that they might be doing "God's Will," they are allowed free will to create far more than humans believe. If they had no free will, there would be no duality. If there was no duality, then God would not have a complete reflection of all of His possibilities. Free will plays a role in our choosing, and without knowledge we cannot choose. Without knowledge, we are a victim of fate or causality. We use our knowledge to choose, and free will is activated.

To release victimization, one must be knowledgeable.

If God controlled everything then there would be no point to creation. God gave free will to the beings of this universe so that He might know the possibility of his own creations. God knows Himself through His creations (all of us), and we know ourselves through our creations.

All of us, in a human vessel, experience the impact of duality. We live because of the pull of gravity, and because of this we know our feet as down, and our heads as up. We divide the day into night and day. Those who experience extended periods of all light, or all dark, find the experience to be disorienting. Without the division of nighttime to establish us within a new day, humans float from one day into the next with little awareness that a new day is begun. If 3 a.m. and 7 a.m. look exactly like 12 p.m., and it repeats for a long period of time, the natural rhythms, known as circadian rhythms become confused. Those with no eyesight also lose their circadian rhythms, locked into endless darkness. The drug, *Tasimelteon*, was recently developed to assist those totally blind individuals with a condition called Non-24-sleep-wave disorder. This drug assists the brain to function in a more "normal" wave pattern, helping the individual to sleep.

Duality allows us to lock our five senses into a limited reality and defines every aspect of our world. We have become so dualistic that we have divided almost everything into half. The beginning of non-sex, gender identification, makes many people extremely uncomfortable, as does same-sex marriage. We are locked into a world of opposites, and we were raised to believe, "opposites attract." Yet, what we have noticed is that opposites fight. Opposites create tension; healthy, yes, when kept in a respectful arena, but unhealthy, and dangerous, when it becomes war. Breaking our consciousness out of duality appears to be an enormous task, and we must ask ourselves if too much anarchy in this regard is dangerous as well. Do we need some duality to continue along with creation? How is it to be regulated?

One of my clients recently went into a future life. It was unclear if the life was hundreds or thousands of years in the future, and yet, it appeared to be on the Earth. The world she inhabited had no duality. It was completely peaceful, well-ordered and safe. She sensed that it was run by an enormous consciousness, like a computer, but unlike any computer we could comprehend. Everything was easy. She also said that, "we are forbidden to know anything about the history of the Earth during the years of conflict." Conflict, it appears, can only be eliminated by making sure that it isn't within the consciousness of the general public. She was happy, and she said that there were flowers, trees and other lifeforms upon the Earth. Everything was regulated, but in a way to keep the peace, health and safety for all living things. It sure sounds good, until you wonder how much growth actually takes place in such a life. That thought leads to the next one, "Do we need duality, and conflict, to create?"

Those of you who carry the Samskara (the mental/emotional karmic complex) of being angry at God for creating (or allowing) duality and conflict, might find such a world to your liking. Those of you who like a little, or a lot, of adventure, might find such a place boring.

I have done past life regressions with people for over twenty years, and in-between their lives many people report arguing with their spiritual guides about returning to the Earth. "I don't want to go back," they report saying to their guides. Eventually, it appears, they return. Something continues to draw many of us back into this conflict-ridden dimension of duality, and maybe it isn't all bad. Maybe the growth we achieve while on the Earth contributes to better choices in the future.

The most debated dualistic state of consciousness is the one called: good vs. evil. I have found that the word evil is almost forbidden among intellectuals. Intellectuals appear to be uncomfortable with the idea that the opposite of good is evil. But, I will say, that many of the intellectuals I have met, who purport to feel uncomfortable with the word evil, live relatively comfortable lives, lives where fascism has not (yet) knocked directly upon their door. Anyone who has ever encountered the energy of pure evil…. recognizes it immediately. It falls over you like a veil, and almost stops your heart; it cannot be ignored.

We appear to balk at good vs. evil; and yet, in my opinion, those who are experiencing the horror that is currently overtaking South Sudan (for example) might find it difficult to deny the existence of evil. The saying that the smartest thing the Devil ever did was convincing people he doesn't exist, may well be true. If the Devil does not exist, where do we then put all this darkness that exists on the Earth? For the most part, we ignore what makes us uncomfortable, and evil makes us very uncomfortable. Perhaps like Lucifer and Michael, we don't like the mirror it presents. If we research the number of armed conflicts throughout the world, occurring right this vary minute, it is enormous. The drug wars in Mexico alone killed 15,000 people last year. So, whether we like it or not, evil is very alive on this planet.

Some believe that evil is outside of God. I cannot discover where they believe it sits. Very often they have no answer for that. Some believe evil is just contorted good. Some believe that evil has no consciousness of its own but is merely an expression of a misguided human being. Please ask yourself this question, "Does evil exist within the body of God?" Shamans, who learn to successfully navigate the lower astral realms, recognize the existence of these demonic energies. These are the energies that house within us and turn us into lower beings. They bring us further from our Higher Self, and bring us into a reactionary, fear-based, state of mind. We feed the Devil by creating evil, and the Overlord of Evil is a hungry beast.

Clients of mine who have made dark contracts in other lives

and are trying to free themselves from the chains of their previous actions, report a Dark Overlord who needs to be constantly fed by fear and chaos. This Overlord tortures the servant to create murder and bedlam, and the servant and the master are both fed from the fear of the victim. For a short while, I have been told, the servant feels relief from the constant badgering of the Overlord immediately after the feeding, but soon they are pushed relentlessly to harm again. This Overlord parasite needs constant feeding, and it relies on its servants to keep it fed.

Is this Overlord outside of God? Does it rule a Kingdom equal to God's Kingdom? Or is this Overlord a monster created from the evil deeds of humans and other beings; deeds that have accumulated over billions of years, and eventually took form within the Body of God?

If you believe that God is the One Source, then you are more likely to believe the idea that the Overlord is a monster created from our monstrous acts. If you believe that there is a Kingdom of Evil equal to God's Kingdom of Good, then you see all of reality as a constant state of war...a state of war that will never end as long as there is any creational force left.

For me, Good is the energy of balanced Creation, and Evil is the energy of unbalanced Destruction. Both live within the Kingdom of God, the Source of All. I believe that the push and pull, the duality of good and evil, are both housed within All That Is. I believe that they work best in balance. Creation creates in equal measure with destruction. When these energies get "out of balance," then disease results. Once the balance gets too far to one side or the other, the natural impulse is to re-find a type of homeostasis. In other words, creation and destruction need each other, in a state of balance, to survive.

I do believe in evil as an expression of consciousness. I have felt the energy of evil a few times in my life. It has made its presence known to me, and I believe it has a consciousness and an agenda. Its job is to destroy anything that might create peace, love, joy and happiness...its job is to invert everything. Those infected with evil find that killing creates happiness in them. Those infected with evil enjoy destruction, in fact, *their* energy of creation is a destructive chaos. They create through destruction. Those of you who have done past life regression with me, and faced your own fears and demons, often gain a deeper understanding of the energy of evil. What I hear from those who are brave enough to "go there" is, "I feel so much more empowered now." Facing darkness empowers us. When we stop running and turn to confront the demon chasing us in our dream state, the demon loses power.

Although the original duality was created by the Archangel Michael/Lucifer split, the teams have grown enormously over the many, many, many, years. Absolute power corrupts absolutely, and that might have been said of Lucifer. Although he started out as equal to Michael, his belief that he was indeed better, and more powerful than Michael, began to corrupt his energy. His mind twisted into an inverted shape. He saw himself only as good, and Michael only as bad. He began to believe that his rule should be absolute over all the angelic kingdoms, and that God had appointed him to serve directly under Him, as his sole and true heir.

Those who worship Lucifer still consider him to be the "good" angel. They believe that his Light is the true light, and that he is, by his name, the Lightbearer, appointed by God to rule. These worshippers call themselves Satanists.

Most people think of their Soul Purpose as some grand impact upon the outside world. Rarely do they realize that their soul purpose is with themselves. It is much easier to act outside, than it is to look within. Your soul purpose is to heal your soul. You have no other job than that. Understanding your own relationship to duality, and how it plays out in your life, is the key to healing Michael/Lucifer and their split. The mirror is our friend, and the more you like yourself the easier it is to peer within it. I have clients who have said to me that they can't look in the mirror and say, "I love you," to the image they see there. If you have difficulty with this exercise, the healing of it will be to peer into your own darkness; for it is your dark nature that keeps you from saying those three simple words to yourself. Your shame of your own darkness, holds you prisoner to the Overlord.

CHAPTER FOUR

The Teams Form

Family of Light: A harmonious and creational force. In service to others. It embodies an expansive, open, and sharing energy. Feeds directly from the Light and Love of God. The Family of Light honors free will, and the universal law of karma. They do not intervene unless asked to do so.

Family of Dark: A destructive and chaotic force. In service to self. It embodies a secretive, exclusive energy. Feeds from other humans. Be aware that they can appear to serve others, and fool people, but in the end, they are psychopathic/sociopathic vampires, and serve the self. The Family of Dark attempts to find a way around the universal law of karma by manipulating the person to say, "Yes." They have come to understand that if they get you to agree, or at least not object, to their agenda, they will have no karmic kickback. This is done not because they honor universal law, but because they wish to avoid karma.

Our memories appear to be erased. In fact, lately it seems that people have trouble remembering last week or last year, let alone their soul's history. Are we truly meant to live only "in the now," with no accumulated wisdom or knowledge to benefit our choices? If we understood more than we do, would we actually make choices from love, or is knowledge separate from love? Can people be knowledgeable, or even wise, and yet also be evil? The common belief is that knowledge and wisdom lead inevitably to greater compassion, and that the wise man or woman will behave better than a person who is foolish. But, is that true? Are there beings who know a great deal and yet also lack caring and concern for their fellow man? If you look around you, it appears the answer is, yes.

It might be necessary to rethink some of our old adages; ideas that man is essentially good, or that goodness prevails. Do we cling to the belief that goodness and love will save the day? To be popular, a book or movie must have goodness, or at least fairness somewhere within it, and the hero or anti-hero must save the day in the end. We require a mostly happy ending. We want just enough sadness to make it interesting, but not enough to express hopelessness. In fact, the thing most people fear is not being poor or ill, it's living without hope. And, indeed, humans cannot live without it. Hope is essential to human survival. But, it is because of this very fact, that hope is manipulated. Every despot has realized that if you want someone to work well for you, give them the false hope that their labors will better their position.

We believe that destroying hope is the cruelest thing we can do to another, and so, we continue to give one another hope, whether false or not, as an act of kindness. We say, "There is always hope." However, some people may not know how hope was used against the Jews in the concentration camps. It is well known that a sign above the entrance of Auschwitz (and other camps) read, "Arbeit Macht Frei," meaning "Work makes you free." This was placed there to give the Jews false hope; hope that if they worked hard, the Nazi's would set them free. This kept them working for their enslavers, even though they never intended to liberate them.

Much less well known is the fact that many of the camps had Jewish orchestras used to greet the prisoners as they were let off the trains and brought into the camps. These Jewish musicians were forced to play as part of a ruse to instill false hope in the prisoners as they entered the camps. As one survivor put it, "At first, I thought, how bad can it be, if they are serenading us?"

If we rely on hope, rather than truth, do we cheat ourselves out of action? One must then ask: Does false hope breed passivity?

In modern day America, we have turned the once grim and ugly fairy tales of the brothers Grimm, into a Disneyworld of illusion. Even after decades of "Women's Liberation" in America we throw princess parties for our little girls and pretend that such a thing as being a fairy princess can exist for them. Are we being kind to them? I understand that this type of "fairy princess" worldview is not available to many women; it is, in many ways, expressly American. We believe we deserve...well, everything. We have been raised to feel that we must always strive for perfection, and in some people's minds if you say something, "negative" about the United States you are a traitor, or if you say something negative about the world, you are a "downer."

It appears that we are entirely out of balance, and are struggling to achieve homeostasis both as individuals, and as a collective. Those of you with painful childhoods often spend the rest of your life trying to balance that out, and because of this you might find that you can't deal with any sort of brutal images. If your personal foundation is weak and damaged due to childhood abuse, you will often seek out an escape from the pain. If your foundation is strong you might find yourself capable of looking squarely at harsh reality.

Those who spend their lives as activists: saving whales, horses, cats, children, dogs, lions, monkeys and other living things, are indeed struggling to save themselves at the same time they save others. The need to help others is sometimes a reaction to a difficult childhood, and in my opinion, is always a reaction to one's past life trauma. Social workers and therapists are struggling to heal others, often, as they heal their own wounding. We use beings outside of the self, to heal the self. This turns the energy of anger at the perpetrator into something more noble, yet, if the original wound within the therapist remains too raw, it can create havoc within others. A balanced therapist must be able to bear witness to the suffering of others, see clearly the pain and darkness, and find somewhere to hold it, that isn't within the self. This is why so many therapists and healers must themselves have a therapist and a healer to work with; bringing the pain to light, through sharing it with others, can help it to heal.

We see the world and others, as we are, and we deny in the world what we are afraid of in ourselves.

This hearkens back to the idea that the world is a mirror reflecting back our inner wounding. I must add, however, that *there is caution needed* around this concept. If you fear Charles Manson, because you know he is a mass murderer, you are reacting to an evil energy perceived outside the self. Whether he reflects the evil within you is immaterial when it comes to being safe. If you perceive evil energy around you, the smart thing to do is to recognize it, and remove yourself from it, whenever possible. Learning to perceive evil in the energy field, is as important to perceiving good, when it comes to self-preservation. You can reflect on what it means to you personally after you have reacted to keep yourself safe on the physical or astral plane! Sometimes when you perceive evil in another, its because it is there.

So, what does this have to do with the two teams who formed behind Michael and Lucifer? Everything. In the beginning these teams were *not* labeled The Family of Light and The Family of Dark. That level of duality took eons, but, what first took place was a use of free will. Lucifer, it is said, was the Golden Boy. The reason he attracted the most lost and damaged angels was because they saw in him the God they missed so deeply. These angels felt the sting of the separation from God the most, and they saw in Lucifer, a savior; someone who could reproduce for them the Light they longed for. The lost, lonely, abandoned souls looked to Lucifer for relief from their pain of separation out of the One God; he became their "drug of choice." Like groupies feed a rock-star, these angels fed Lucifer's newly burgeoning ego. Every despot on Earth has risen to power in exactly the same manner. The wounded, frightened, and desperate population reaches for the leader who professes to be the strongest, the one who will lift them out of their misery and back into the "golden world, the good old days." Every time a population has followed such a proclaimed leader, they have fallen along with the supposed savior.

In turn for their devotion, Lucifer made them feel loved and important. He reassured them that God hadn't turned them out, hadn't abandoned them. Instead, he said, God wanted them to serve through his favorite son, Lucifer. "Stay close to me, and I'll give you what you need." He began to fill their heads with talk about how inferior his brother Michael was, and how Michael didn't shine as brightly, and how Michael would lead them astray. Soon the angels began to develop traits that never before had been a part of their nature; they began to puff up their wounded hearts with thoughts of "being better than," and "closer to God." (All of you will recognize the rise of Hitler, and the Nazi party, with those ideas.)

Lucifer's angels looked to the legions that had begun to form around Michael and they filled their heads with darker and darker thoughts about the other angels. As they formed these thoughts, they began to densify. Or, to put it in the biblical sense, they began to fall. Dark thoughts and words hold a lower vibration than the vibration of love, and they densify the vessel.

This was, of course, exactly opposite of what they were told would happen to them if they aligned with Lucifer. These fallen angels were "cast out," meaning that their vibrational frequency became denser, lower, and darker. It is for that reason that they became known as the Family of Dark, or the Forces of Darkness, because they were the first to fall further from the Light of God, into a dark and dense world wrought with fear and sadness.

It is, at this time, that Archangel Michael became known as the Prince of Light, and leader of the forces of Light. He was now

Lighter, meaning he vibrated at a higher level, than his brother, Lucifer. His energy grew, while Lucifer's light diminished. That is why today he is known as the leader of the Family of Light.

The confusion over why the Prince of Darkness bears the name of Lucifer (Lightbearer) has left many people to scratch their heads. Perhaps now it makes more sense.

As Lucifer began to densify, his body began to resemble that of a dragon's body. His wings, which previously had shone and glimmered in the light, began to shine with the scales of a reptile, and his words, that had previously had so much power, began to manifest as flame or fire out of his mouth. He began to be known as the Great Dragon and is still known as this today. There was a war in heaven, declares the bible, and Michael fought the Dragon.

Because we love duality so much, we cling to the belief that there is a good angel named Michael and a bad angel named Lucifer. We want it to be clear and clean and we want to know who and what we stand behind. Only those with childish minds see the world that clearly divided between good and evil, black and white. With the battle in heaven, came another state of consciousness, and it is best described with the simple idea: the world began to include shades of gray.

Where previously the angelic realm had existed within the same vibrational band, or dimension of consciousness, it now spread out. The proverbial fall from heaven, or fall from grace, happened as consciousness began to densify and create new worlds of reality. Close to God's womb, and free from fear and anger, the angels felt safe; but now they felt confused and lost. They ventured further and further from their original home. With each thought and action, a new world began to spring up. A new dimension of possibility grew beneath the last dimension. If we imagine that God exists in the twelfth dimension, and the first angelic beings exist in eleventh dimension, it is a long way down to the lower astral realms of the third and fourth dimension; the dimensions that humans occupy.

Was it inevitable that these lower realms be created? Was it only a matter of time before pure creational energy began to manifest emotions that reflect fear and hate? Do we need this push/pull to be active and alive?

Even today, those who team up behind Lucifer often feel powerless without his dark promises. Modern-day Satanists cast spells and harm others to feed this perverted Overlord. Perpetrators often speak of the power rush they feel when they harm another. It is a drug.

But, because there are shades of gray within all of us (some more than others) we have the potential to do kindness, as well as harm. Within every saint is a sinner, and within every sinner lives a saint. We are given, at every moment, the opportunity to "sell our soul," as Jesus was tempted by the Devil. Our wounds goad us (as they goaded the original followers of Lucifer in heaven) to puff ourselves up above our fellow man, and to declare ourselves "better than." Our minds keep us trapped in this lower astral hell. We are no different than the original angels. Our wars are their wars.

It is said that man didn't start these wars, but he fights them. I agree, as I believe we are all continuing to fight the ancient war. The war between the angels.

CHAPTER FIVE

Other Cultures Speak
To Our History

The history I speak of is, of course, ancient, and it mirrors the history of the beings we call the Titans and the gods they beget in Mount Olympus. I must continue to remind the reader that every culture, and time period, speaks of powerful beings who sprang directly from Source. The Titans were the Elder Gods and they ruled the universe prior to the better-known Olympians. The Titans are immortal beings of tremendous strength and power. In Greek mythology, they are the personification of the Earth and the Sky. The original Titans are one male and one female: Gaea (Earth) and Uranus (Heaven). They bore children, and the next generation of Titans contain six males, and six females. The most famous of these is Cronos, who turned against his father, and with the help of his brothers and his mother castrated Uranus (his father) and took his place as ruler of the heavens.

Eventually, as these brothers and sisters bred with one another they created children. Zeus, arguably the most famous of the Titan lineage, along with his brothers and sisters, Hades, Hera, Poseidon, Hestia, and Demeter, fought the elder Titans in a battle for dominance. This battle became known as the Titanomachy;

a ten-year long war (I suspect that is in "god years.") They called themselves the Olympian Gods and took over rulership of the Cosmos and the Earth. Crius, a Titan who took over rulership of the heavens, looks an awful lot like Archangel Michael in many depictions. Perhaps Crius is the original Michael/Lucifer before they split apart and fought over ownership of the heavens.

I have worked with clients who believe that they are in direct lineage of these Titans; the energy is enormous and difficult to handle. The clients I have worked with are both struggling to contain the power and have gone into hiding. It appears they are trying to hide from their vengeful brothers and sisters. I see all of these energies and stories as similar. Angels, Extradimensionals, Extraterrestrials, Titans, and the gods of all cultures share something in common; they share the ability to manipulate the environment well beyond the average human. They can materialize, and dematerialize at will, for example.

In Chinese mythology there are the Eight Immortals. These beings have supernatural powers, and Zhang Guolao, a famous immortal, has many abilities attributed to him that are superhuman.

Other examples of ancient theories, that differ from the norm, include Sigmund Freud's theory that Moses was actually a follower of the Egyptian pharaoh, Akhenaten, and learned monotheism from Akhenaten. Others believe that Akhenaten was Extraterrestrial (including myself), and Graham Hancock, author of *Fingerprints of the Gods*, has published on his website the belief that Akhenaten and Moses are indeed the same person. This would make Moses an Extraterrestrial, and the technology he used to part the Red Seas, extraterrestrial technology. Both of these theories make Moses an Egyptian, not Hebrew, and certainly if you dig more deeply you see many interesting points of view around these issues.

Akhenaten is depicted with an elongated skull, and it has been written that he wanted himself portrayed as lifelike. This would make him an Annunaki. I, for one, have no trouble believing this because I have uncovered my own past life with blue skin, and an elongated skull. In that life, it was my job to move between the spaceships and *The City of Gods*, also known as Teotihuacan, Mexico. I would transport myself from the spaceships through a portal at the top of the Pyramid of the Sun and inform the priest of the latest news around the Orion Wars. When I visited Teotihuacan, I remembered many aspects of my past life visits to that most holy extraterrestrial city. It appears my modern day need to inform readers of these ancient wars, is linked to that past life. The word angel means messenger, and the (UFO) ships that transported me (and others) place-to-place to deliver these communications were called Messenger Ships. If Archangel Gabriel is the "angelic messenger," could he be the commander and leader of these ships?

Those of you who believe you are an ancient soul, will remember these theories deep within your subconscious mind. If you don't feel "whole," or know the answer to the question, "who am I?" it is often because your soul's memories don't match up with the belief systems of the culture you were raised within. I understand that much of what I write has a Judeo-Christian point of view; that's the culture I am surrounded by. However, even the story of the Great Flood, that beset Noah, is found not only in the Old Testament, but in civilizations around the world. Here is a sampling of the other cultures and civilizations who have within their "mythology" a Great Flood story: Sumer, India, China, Philippines, Hawaiian, Hopi, Incan, Korean, and so many more. So, although I might speak of Noah's flood, I am well aware that it is not a culturally-owned story. So too, is it with these tales of war between the angels (or gods as some people call them.) Each religion and culture relate the story in their own way, and with their own point of view.

What's important isn't who is right, instead, it is the fact that these ideas are worldwide and live deep within the subconscious of many, many people. Modern science, and modern religion, have attempted to eradicate mystical ancient theories, but have been only partially successful. This knowledge is deeper than one lifetime of re-programming, and those who hold this knowledge, find it scratches at the wall modern man has erected to keep our deep wisdom at bay.

Even today, stories abound of experiences with Extraterrestrial/ Extradimensional beings who can materialize and dematerialize and change shape. These beings have technology that sounds like Zeus' lightning bolts, or Poseidon's ability to create tsunamis. If you are aware of America's modern technologies, you will see a similar ability in DARPA's (the military's invention wing) ability to create devices to "disappear" objects and people, and project holograms. The gods are giving us their technology, and like the gods, we allow our lower minds to rule with this power. We currently use our god-like technologies to gain more power over others. Modern alien abductees tell the same story over and over; the story of "gods" with powers greater than humans. Powers that allow them to move through walls and lift people from their beds.

I must insert something here: On the internet there are many people who will state that <u>all</u> psychic attack is from the military and dark-op projects. They insist that all targeting is this. They also believe that all channeling is from the dark-op military. Although there is a great deal of this going on, we must remember that psychic attacks have been going on for millennia, long before our governments learned how to reproduce psychic attack with weapons. Psychic attack is both energetic and military.

There are others who believe that all targeting is demonic or from the Grays or the Reptilians. They believe that all channeling is done from them. Then there are those who believe that all channeling is from a Divine Source. I want people to understand that although psychic attack targeting can be coming from human, third-dimensional, sources, it can also be from other dimensional sources as well. It is not true that all channeling is good, or bad. The goal is to work from ones Higher Self, after all. Anything can be used to enlighten or deceive, and it is important that you remain open-minded when discussing these issues!

There is an old tale about each blind man holding a different part of the elephant, and when asked what an elephant looks like, they describe what their own hands have landed upon. Whether someone is speaking on your television about the day's news, or about metaphysical topics, its best to avoid polarizing extremes, and remain open to new ideas before judging.

In order to understand such complex concepts and ideas, we must simplify them. It is important to have a grasp of these ideas because instead of this history being further from our modern lives, it is closer. Thousands of stories of abductions are documented. John E. Mack, who was a professor of psychiatry at Harvard Medical School, and later became a devoted believer in the phenomenon, and David M. Jacobs, the professor at Temple University, who spent much of his career documenting the stories of abductees, are merely two of the many who have believed, and continue to believe, that Extraterrestrial/Extradimensional beings are deeply involved in our modern world.

As I mentioned previously, Lucifer's fall into density created the lower dimensions, and into these dimensions fell his crew of angels. Instead of feeling closer to the Light and God, they became more and more afraid, and their fear led them to manifest emotions that were indeed new to them: anger, jealousy, guilt, shame. They began to lash out at one another, and the lower astral realm grew. It filled with shades of gray energy. The shades range from black to a light gray. The Christians call it purgatory or hell, the Buddhists and the Hindus call it Naraka.

Within this hell there are many levels. The consciousness, and deeds, of the individual soul determines the level of hell into which he/she manifests. For Buddhists, a Naraka is not just one thing. To the Buddhists the Naraka is divided into many levels including the division into Hot and Cold. What is interesting in reading the definitions of Naraka, is that many of the tortures endured by those trapped in a Naraka resemble human forms of torture perfected on Earth. Human beings, with the help of demonic energies, have brought the Naraka tortures to the Earth, and have used them on one another. Are torture chambers run by the "demons" who were trapped in the Naraka, and then escaped their prison to bring the torture they endured to the Earth? Do humans, infected by these distorted demonic energies, become vessels for their dark tortures, and dark thoughts?

For Buddhists, there also exists another realm called the Bardo. The Bardo is often described as where the soul goes between lives. The recognition that consciousness creates reality upon death is well understood by those who believe in Bardo states. In my experience, the departing soul creates its own experiences. For example, recently, during a past life regression a client remembered going into a gray zone and reincarnating quickly from that place after a medieval life of war, and then transcending into the highest states of heaven after life as a healer (even though the death in that life came through persecution.) It appears to me, over many years of this type of work, that indeed there are many states of consciousness created by a soul.

We do, indeed, create our own hell. Many of those, who are trapped within a hell realm of their own making, manifest jealousy, envy, shame, guilt, and other emotions that eat away at the soul. Forgiveness releases one from anger, and the reason to do it is for the self. The anger keeps you trapped in hell, but to forgive releases you from hell.

The angels, who resided in the higher realms of light, felt sorry for the fallen ones. These were their brothers and sisters and they wanted them to be happy again. *They wanted to save them.* Human-incarnated Angels of Light have this emotional complex. They want to save the ones trapped in darkness. First, and foremost, they don't understand why anyone would want to be trapped in hell realm, and they make the assumption that if someone is there they don't want to be there. So, it was with the Angels of Light and the beings who had become known as the Legions of Michael. They looked "down" at the fallen angels and assumed that those beings just needed a hand up, and that they would be given gratitude for the helping hand and reunited in love once again. Wrong.

The Angels of Light didn't realize what darkness does to consciousness. It starts to "feel good," to be down there. It starts to be enjoyable to think you are better than others, and that you know more, and to be in a constant state of judgment. The Angels of Light (not sharing that consciousness) didn't understand how the egos of the fallen ones had come into being. The egos (or individuated consciousness) became the dark side of creation, whispering lies and half-truths into the ears of the fallen ones.

The Sumerian tale of: *The Descent of Inanna,* describes perfectly what the Angels of Light experienced in trying to save their fallen brothers and sisters. Inanna, known as the *Queen of Heaven,* is dressed in her finest: a crown, necklace, golden ring, and scepter, when she chooses to descend into the Underworld to rescue her fallen sister, Ereshkigal. She gives instructions to her servant, Ninsubur, of how to come to her aid, should she fail to return from the Underworld. Upon the gates of the Underworld, Inanna knocks loudly and demands entrance. Neti, the Chief Gatekeeper, inquires as to her name. "I am Inanna, the Queen of Heaven, and I demand you let me in," she says. Neti replies, "Why would you want to come to the place from which no traveler returns?"

"Because of my sister," replies Inanna.

When Neti informs Ereshkigal (Inanna's sister) of Inanna's presence at the gate, Ereshkigal is not pleased. Instead of offering Inanna entrance she demands that Inanna be stopped at seven gates, and that at each one she be required to give up her possessions and her clothing. When Inanna asks why, she is told by Neti, "Quiet, Inanna, the ways of the Underworld are perfect."

Inanna enters Ereshkigal's throne room, bowed low, naked and afraid.

> *"The annuna, the judges of the Underworld, surrounded her*
> *They passed judgement against her.*

Ereshkigal fastened upon Inanna, the eye of death.
She spoke against her, the word of wrath
She uttered against her the cry of guilt
She struck her.
Inanna was turned into a corpse
A piece of rotting meat
And was hung from a hook on the wall."

When Inanna does not return, her servant, with the assistance of Enki, (Inanna's father and the most powerful of all in heaven), sends demons to rescue her. The demons enter the Underworld, like flies, and attach themselves to Ereshkigal, causing her great distress. She asks the demons what it will take for them to stop punishing her, and they answer as Enki instructed them to, "We want only the corpse rotting on the wall (Inanna.) Thus, Inanna was revived and brought out from the Underworld.

Most modern readers will interpret tales like *Persephone's Journey into Hades*, and *The Descent of Inanna* into hell, as depictions of the four seasons. We are told that each of these stories is a parable of summer, fall, winter and the ascent is the spring. It was the ancient people's way of expressing the four seasons. Could we not also understand this "fable" in another way?

Why is it that, most likely, every human-incarnated Angelic Being of Light has experienced something very similar to Inanna? I hear these stories over and over. Why is it that we have introduced the idea of "co-dependency" into organizations like AA, in the attempt to teach others not to "save?" The lesson we must learn is to stop saving those who don't want to be saved, and if we jump into the Underworld with our sisters and brothers we will be hung on a hook and wind up like Inanna. Each soul, we begin to learn, must rescue themselves. They must reach up from the Underworld and do the work to lift their mind, body and spirit from hell. We must be like the Lighthouse on the shore and shine our Light without jumping into the muddy water. If we jump in, we both drown.

CHAPTER SIX

The Family Of Light And The Family Of Dark

When Lucifer brought the angels to the lower dimensions with him, it felt to these angels that they were cut-off from God all together. Before the fall, the angels had fed from the Source, or God's Light, and they used it to fuel their energetic bodies. It is for that reason that angels are depicted with wings, halos, and bodies of Light. As they lost their connection to God they began to feed from each other. Today we call this the act of an energy vampire. Instead of proper feeding from God's Source of Light, while on the Earth, most people feed from other people. To weaken a person, and make it easier to feed from them, we create control dramas.

A famous book, *The Celestine Prophecy*, by James Redfield, labels these control dramas and explains them in detail. The four methods, he defines, that people use to feed from one another are: *Interrogators* (threaten others), *Intimidators* (judge and question others), *Aloof behavior* (drawing energy by remaining distant and mysterious), and *Poor Me's* (victims who make us feel responsible for their problems.) When we engage in these behaviors we drain energy, or Chi, from the person we are attacking. It is one of the reasons many people don't believe that two people can succeed equally; they see the success of another person as their loss. We see one as "up" and well fed, while we believe that the other must be "starving," and hence, they are the loser. If we fed properly, from God, we would realize that there is enough energy to go around for all people, equally.

If the light of the soul is dim, due to lower consciousness, the human being will be confused about the idea of feeding from God. They won't understand how to close their eyes and draw Light from Source to fill them up. In fact, it is possible they will feel the idea is completely foreign to them. This is the state that humans find themselves in today. Like the fallen angels, they feel cut off from God's Light, and like the angels, must create control dramas to feed from one another. When the control drama becomes severe it becomes evil. When it becomes evil, it becomes The Family of Dark.

THE BLACK SUN, the FALSE GOD, JESUS and ASHTAR of the FAMILY OF DARK

Because the Family of Dark takes the good and makes it bad,

and because the third dimensional, lower astral plane is wedded to duality, there has existed on planet Earth, representations of both a "Good God," and an "Evil God." The Family of Dark has created an oppositional energy to the positive expression most of you are familiar with. This picture is SS Nazi, Heinrich Himmler's, representation of the Black Sun; in direct opposition to the sun we all know and love. It is found in Heinrich Himmler's, Wewelsburg castle. In my opinion, the fact that it is believed Heinrich Himmler had it installed in the floor of the room they called, "The Hall of the Supreme General's," depicts the Family of Dark perfectly. Invert everything good and make it evil. Like the Swastika, the Sonnenrad, or Black Sun symbol, was taken from ancient cultures and used for the purpose of energizing the Nazi party's agenda.

The false God is the one to whom we perform sacrifices. In the "olden days," the sacrifices were human. If you research it (even a little bit online) you will see every ancient culture has performed human sacrifice to appease their God. This God, that people feared, was a false Reptilian god that needed to be fed with human fear-based energy and blood. The Aztec god of war and sacrifice was named, Huitzilopochtli, and his shrine, on top of the pyramid Tenochtitlan, was decorated with skulls and red paint to represent blood.

Before Jesus tried to stop the practice, human sacrifice was practiced for thousands of years before it was lessened to animal sacrifice. Children and maidens were slaughtered to feed this Dark Overlord that people called "God." After feeding people to God was looked down upon, or even prohibited, (except during wartime, where we consider it an honor to be slaughtered) the human race turned to goats, sheep and other livestock. That God is a Reptilian god designed to fool the masses.

Recently, in London, seven people were murdered in a terrorist attack. Some people's throats were slashed in a restaurant, and others were mowed down on London bridge. Two separate eyewitnesses told the press that the attackers cried out, "This is for Allah!" If you do some research you will realize that many people are still performing sacrifices in their own way. How else can you interpret an event such as this?

Not only has God been turned into a God who needs blood to be fed, but the Family of Dark also co-opted Jesus. The Romans crucified Jesus (there are those who truly believe he was not crucified, and I am open to that idea, but it is not currently my truth due to my experiences during that time in history) and thought that would be the end of it. After all, every other Messiah the Romans had crucified (and there were many) is lost to history. But, long after Jesus was crucified, the remaining disciples were still preaching his words, so the Family of Dark knew that something needed to be done.

The Roman Empire is a perfect expression of a Draconian Reptilian world; for example, the way they would torture people in large arenas for public pleasure. (Talk about feeding a Dark Overlord.) Family of Dark, Reptilian ETs, figured if they couldn't kill the "real Jesus," they could create a false Jesus that required sacrifice of money and power to a greater church and they did this by showing the man, Saul, (aka Paul) a visionary hologram in the sky of Jesus. This event is documented in Saul/Paul's own words. He believed he was seeing a vision of the real Jesus in the sky. They then implanted thoughts in his head that led him to believe he knew Jesus better than the disciples, even though Saul never met Jesus.

The Reptilians believed it was Saul's job was to bring Jesus back to Rome and bring him under Roman control. The historical Jesus worked to free the Jews from Rome, but the modern Jesus resides there. There is a reason so much killing and pedophilia has been done in the name of the Roman Catholic religion; at its heart, the Roman church is still tied to the Reptilian god, or the false God. The real Jesus champions love, forgiveness, and the "God within," not power and control over others. The reason the church asks you to "eat the body of Christ," and consume "his blood," as a holy sacrament is because it mimics the "old dark ways" of feeding God. (By the way: it is through Saul where I believe the Reptilian hologram comes in, not during the crucifixion, as others believe.)

Well, enter the New Age; the age we all live in. We are supposed to be awake and enlightened, and yet we still get tricked by "Hansel and Gretel candy houses" or spiritual centers that were set up in the New Age to lure in the innocent with sweet, sugar-coated, candy words. The newest form of entrapment appears to be in the form of the Ashtar Commander and the Galactic Federation. It's not that there aren't "good ETs/EDs," but since humanity is completely naïve when it comes to Extraterrestrial or Extradimensional alien life, it's very easy to construct false ETs to fool people.

In online renditions, the Ashtar Commander is depicted as a Nordic Pleiadean extraterrestrial, with white skin, blond hair, blue-eyes, a very angelic-like being here to rescue the human race. However, it appears that if there is a good Ashtar, available to humanity, he is long gone, being replaced by, once again, a false Ashtar. I have read that the Gray aliens can alter their appearance to mimic a blond, blue-eyed

I have encountered a number of people who have been tricked by this false Galactic Ashtar. The worst case, I have encountered, is a woman who thought she was making a contract with the good Ashtar to be used for the Light when, in fact, she was abducted by the dark side. Ever since she meditated with "him," and gave him permission to use her body as an instrument of "light," she has been hearing voices in her head that tell her if she continues to do her healing work she will be killed. She informed me that she remembers making the vow, being taken into a spaceship, and then blacked out. She has no memory of anything else until she awoke in her own home, hearing voices in her head that torment her with threats. She is not alone. These targeted individuals have been tricked into dark contracts with beings that they thought were "good." There are many websites devoted to helping targeted individuals. I list some of them in Part Two.

Those of you interested in implants should check out the documentary entitled *Patient Seventeen*. It is available online. What amazed me about this documentary is how Patient Seventeen will talk about the Gray alien visitations he had as a child, call these beings the "criminals of the alien world," go to a doctor who specializes in implant removal, and then struggle to accept the diagnosis that the material of the implant is of non-human making. This is primarily because total acceptance of the experiences he has had make him feel like an "odd-ball" in society. He feels he can't integrate the truth of his reality, with the reality of the people around him. This illustrates how hard it is to be "different" than the "norm."

Another equally compelling story, and far more detailed, is the Terry Lovelace account of abduction and implantation. He is a 64-year-old former Assistant Attorney General who has "come out of the closet" with his book entitled, *Incident at Devil's Den, a True Account by Terry Lovelace*. His experiences are chilling, but anyone who wants to understand these experiences fully should include his book in their research. Interviews are also available online. Physical implants often grow cysts around them, as the body attempts to expel the foreign object. In Terry's case the implant had two wires attached to it that appear to interface with his nervous system.

The danger is that once a person has been implanted, and they begin to hear voices, they are ruled "insane." Or, in another scenario, the individual trusts the voices and guidance, which leads the person into ruin. It is possible that family members and friends will turn against them. If they are sent to a psychiatrist often they are over medicated to keep them even further repressed and powerless. Rule #1 in the Family of Dark playbook: divide and conquer. Rule #2: make the good/bad and the bad/good. Rule #2 has tricked many people over the last few thousands of years.

Tricking and manipulating human beings is what the Family of Dark specializes in, and they have grown quite good at it. An example of this, especially in light of Russian interference in so many aspects of Western society, is indicated in the following video. In a YouTube video, taken from a 1984 interview, an ex-KGB propaganda agent named Yuri Bezmenov, who later defected, describes how he was used by the Russian government to influence the West. (To locate this interview, you can Google: Yuri Bezmenov interview). This included professors, politicians, businessmen, and even New Age gurus. He calls them, "useful idiots." It is interesting that in the section which runs from 49:55 to 54:09 into the video, he describes how the teachings of gurus, to "drop out of society," and "just meditate," was useful to Russia, because it kept people away from caring about society's ills.

Today we call it the New Age. Be only in the now, don't look at the bad stuff, "it's all good." These are propaganda tools, that can be used to keep us in the narcissistic mindset, we are all a part of. The most frightening example I encountered was in a healing workshop I attended where a participant announced she had, "Nothing to learn from history," because she lived only in the now. If she was truly enlightened, she would realize that her past is with her today, and her karmic consciousness is *alive in the past and the present*. If you can't learn from your past, you are destined to keep repeating the same mistakes. That benefits those who want to keep you enslaved, but not those who want you to wake up!

Those of you susceptible to following "false gurus" need to step back and take a look at why. Often, we long so much for a community, that we will join up with a group of people who appear to offer us salvation. Why is that the human race continually falls for religious and spiritual cults, that empower the leaders and disempower the followers? Why is it that we believe God is outside of us? And, why is it that time and time again, another cult leader rises up and another group of people follow him/her? It appears that we are powerless to change this behavior. Our wounds are so deep that we find it impossible to believe that God is within all of us.

People who study the life of Jesus often come to realize that it was his intention to empower those around him; and he shunned wealth and celebrity. Remember what Jesus told you, "The Kingdom of God lies within." Stop reaching out to false prophets; those who have to change their names to something like Starfeather Lightbeing. Many of these people request an enormous sum to connect you to Jesus or another ascended master, and they make sure you know that you are "beneath" them. If you don't believe that you are worthy enough to be in direct communion, my suggestion is you figure out why. You and Jesus have every right to commune, without outside interference.

Chances are, if you are reading this book, you wouldn't be tricked by a televangical preacher, or fire and brimstone preacher, so why are you in the same old paradigm of believing that you must give your power away to another to be saved? The real Jesus never told you that you were worthless, or less than, or that you needed to give money to the corrupted preachers. He said, "This and more shall ye do," that's how much he believed that you had the power of God within you, just as he had it within himself. He is the son of God, and you are the son/daughter of God. In my opinion, we are all the sons and daughters of God. Jesus met the trials associated with becoming an Ascended Master; he became free of fear.

VAMPIRES AND WITCHES

Modern-day vampires and witches come from the Angelic/Starseed lineage. The most powerful witch might be said to be Hecate, the Greek goddess who rules over witchcraft, sorcery, and all magical knowledge. She embodies what most practicing witches would love to have: power over sky and earth, and all the elements. The Craft comes from the longing to manipulate the natural world to one's desire. Where, in the purest sense, it is the utilizing of herbs and nature in reverence, witches and wizards must always watch out for the ego attachment to the outcome. The casting of spells grew from the longing to use the energy of the Earth goddess to assist women to empower themselves, especially in a very patriarchal world.

Many modern-day witches are "good witches," and their impulse to join with a coven comes from a desire to be with others who understand their point of view. Using the Craft for good purposes can bring one into greater harmony with the natural world; and many witches have had lifetimes where they communed with the elemental world, as clearly as most people talk to other humans. Many witches used herbs to treat other women in need, during the dark ages. These uses of witchcraft are for healing purposes, and a truly "good witch" would never use their power against another human being and curse them. Unfortunately, when human ego gets involved human beings are capable of almost anything.

I have heard of Reiki circles being used to cast spells and curse others. That is not what the energy of Reiki is intended to do, yet, many people fall into the trap of dark power through the wrong use of will, and use even a healing energy, such as Reiki, for dark magic.

Casting spells becomes less necessary when you work in conjunction with your angelic nature, and have faith in your Higher Self, or your God Self, or God, to guide you where it is you need to be. The moment one's thoughts merge with the Higher Self, one often thinks twice before casting a spell. Using spells to get what you want, whether it is money, a man or woman, or a better job, is inserting the lower ego-mind into the mix, and it interferes with the Higher Self. Try letting go and letting God and see what happens. Most modern-day witches are of Starseed and angelic origin, and they have had gifts since childhood, or in other lifetimes. But, disempowered humans longing to have power, can misuse the craft and invite dark energies to mingle with them. These humans might slip into dark magic, because it lures them with power. But, be aware, dark magic boomerangs. Always.

Vampires are coming out of the closet. If you doubt me watch the video on a FOX 5 newscaster interviewing a vampire; and acting like nothing is weird. Go onto YouTube and insert in the Search bar: *Man forecloses on Wells Fargo bank Fox 5 News*. (I hope it will still be available upon publication, because the man has enormous fangs, not just shaved teeth, and the interviewer pretends that he doesn't. It's quite odd, and amazing!)

This modern-day vampire with fangs isn't hiding his identity. The

New York Post just ran an article on two modern day vampires; one sucks blood, the other energy. Vampire Barbie? Oh, Yes. Also, vampire Barbie makeup for kids. On the YouTube channel, it encourages kids to CLICK IF YOU LOVE VAMPIRES. *Twilight* and other television series and movies lure young adults into the vampire world. And, most people think it is a myth. Think again. I have worked with human clients who have been turned in other lifetimes. They carry the vampire signature and struggle to release themselves from it. In my opinion, the vampires are a mixture of Pleiadean/angelic/Reptilian DNA. That gives them power, but at a price; in order to truly "turn" someone their DNA must be altered as well, however, some vampires claim that they can turn someone easily. The lure for children and young adults is power and abilities beyond the mortal. Feeling special and powerful is a state of mind that many humans desperately need. *The Historian,* by Elizabeth Kostova, is an exciting novel that blends fact and fiction to explore the truth about Vlad Dracula.

WHAT IS A SOUL: Can It Be Manufactured?

Does a dog have a soul? Catholics have told me they were raised to believe that animals don't have a soul. Hindus revere the cow as sacred, and give it the status of a god, but, Americans slaughter cows and abuse them without thinking twice about it. Why? Why is it that certain cultures treat animals differently? Why do the Chinese have a Dog Meat day of celebration, and slaughter thousands of dogs and eat them on a day of celebration, while Americans are horrified? Why is it okay to kill some beings, and yet not others? In order to define evil, you must be clear about why you feel the way you do about killing…either animals, or even humans. Is it okay to abort a baby, yet you hate the death penalty? Do you have no problem eating pigs, but are horrified at eating dogs? Again, we can say it is cultural, but, why is it that we don't even agree on the nature of the soul?

One might ask: Why are we so lost in the lower astral realms that we can't even recognize the existence of a soul? Are you certain that you could recognize a soulless human? The robots are getting so lifelike it is difficult to distinguish one from an actual human. Sex robots are being manufactured in American factories by the thousands. Could someday, in the perfected state, such a robot fool you? Some people believe they are actually walking around today, among the "regular" population, and yet, few are able to call them out. Have you ever looked into someone's eyes and seen nothing staring back at you? Have you ever looked into someone's eyes and wondered who or what was looking back?

To me, a soul is constructed of many tiny particles of God, arranged to create consciousness. The soul is a precious bit of God's Light that allows us to find our way back Home to the Highest Realms. I believe that animals have souls. I believe that many animals share a soul group and have a connection to that soul group. When a scientist clones a sheep with a cow, and creates a new un-ensouled animal, in my opinion, it is very dangerous and unkind to the animal. Reports by my clients during past life regression, are that in Atlantis the mixing of DNA was done quite often; humans were mixed with oxen, for example, to make them stronger as slaves. The end result was an oxen/human with strength, yet enough reasoning, to make simple, but important decisions in the workplace.

All the depictions of beings that are half-human and half-animal, in every culture, throughout the ancient world, tell the story of these Atlantean half-breeds. The manner in which we play with DNA today is in no way new to the Earth. Every time a culture develops its scientific capability beyond its mental/emotional/spiritual consciousness it annihilates itself. It is, in my opinion, inevitable.

Are these half-breeds ensouled? When they die, what happens to them? Do they wander the astral plane looking for a soul group? We must have greater clarity of our spiritual nature if we are going to play God.

In my previous book, *Merlin's War: The Battle Between the*

Family of Light and the Family of Dark, I speak of creator gods who are doing what our scientists are doing today. I talk about how the creator gods are battling over the two main templates: the Reptilian template, and the human template. If you believe the bible when it calls Lucifer the Dragon, then you won't find it such a stretch to think that the Reptilian template, or the Draconian Reptilian ETs, come from his team.

These powerful creator gods are not only responsible for other lifeforms, but they created the original Holy Grail, and other powerful objects. When we see Archangel Michael carrying a sword, we must realize that it is not, in any way, shape or form, a human sword. The only words the ancient people had to describe what they saw in his hands was the word sword. But, Michael's sword is a multi-dimensional laser, designed to protect and fight in the astral plane. It is the same with wings. Although the wings are actual streams of energetic light pulsing off the body of the angelic being; humans depict them as wings because that is what they know. If we are to truly break through the old stories and teachings into something that speaks to our deeper truth, we must be willing to see in new ways.

What is the Holy Grail? There are references to such a thing in pagan literature, and other cultures mention a powerful and holy weapon or artifact of power. From the Egyptians to King Arthur, and the legend of the Sword in the Stone, mankind has repeated "myths" of powerful objects that only the purest or righteous may hold or touch. These depictions are not made up, and although modern scientists are attempting to reproduce these weapons, we continually relegate their existence to mythic status.

The Holy Grail is an object of great power. Because of this, it has been fought over since its inception. Knowledge of creation is held in the Grail, and it is what allowed Jesus (as a Grail holder) to turn water into wine, for example. In a sense, he who controls the Grail, controls creation. Our scientists who mix and stir DNA, are trying to break the Grail's code. Although they have not been able to create life from "nothing," they can alter lifeforms by recombining DNA. Just recently they combined human and pig DNA; you can see the resulting fetus online.

Each of these powerful "heavenly" weapons are desired by the Family of Dark and guarded by the Family of Light. However, these weapons have, at certain periods, changed teams. When the Family of Dark can't get their hands upon the original they reconstruct it. It is said that the Philosopher's Stone was the attempt to recreate the Holy Grail. The Stone was used in alchemy, to turn mercury, or lead, to gold. It is said to offer the user immortality (or at least long life.)

We created the nuclear bomb in such a manner, and it serves no one but the Family of Dark. The Family of Light is kept busy trying to keep it from being activated. If the atomic bomb was used extensively enough, it would result in the complete and total annihilation of the human soul template on the Earth's surface.

Yes, I said, human soul template. Nuclear bombs have the potential to fragment the god particle within our bodies. Because these atom bombs release vast quantities of energy from a small amount of matter, if one is directly hit by an atomic bomb it stands to reason that the soul could fragment as well. It is not a weapon that any ensouled human being should desire.

Many of you reading this will disagree with me; you will not believe that the atom bomb could fragment the human soul, and I respect that. However, in over twenty years of doing past life regression I have yet to meet someone who said, "I died in the atomic blast in Hiroshima." (Or Nagasaki.) I am not talking about a slow death after the blast, I am talking about being in the center of the detonation. So, do what you will with this information.

It is interesting to add that Elon Musk has stated that he believes the AI agenda is more dangerous to human existence than even the nuclear bombs.

CHAPTER SEVEN

The War In Heaven Lands On Earth

You can lose many battles and still win the war. As the battle between the angels (or gods) grew more sophisticated, the individual teams (Family of Light and Family of Dark) began to develop weapons which allowed them to attack and defend. The Family of Dark concentrated on weapons of attack, while the Family of Light concentrated on two things: defense and the protection of knowledge.

Understanding that electrons respond to thought and behave differently when they are being viewed, helps us to understand ET technology and such things as the Holy Grail; or Jesus' ability to manipulate solid matter. If you are interested in reading more about this, please research: *Quantum Theory Demonstrated: Observation Affects Reality*, (Weizman Institute of Science, February 27, 1998.) What these experiments proved is that electrons are forced to behave like particles, not waves, by the mere act of observation. Our viewing of an electron alters it from the state of a wave, into a particle. That understanding changes the nature of reality profoundly.

I cannot recommend highly enough that you listen to the Linda Moulton Howe presentation on the simulated universe. It is one of the most enlightening presentations on the nature of reality that

I've heard. *YouTube search: Linda Moulton Howe: Is Our Universe Someone Else's Computer Simulation? on the Ozark Mountain Publishing Channel.*

The Holy Grail falls into the category of the protection of knowledge, because it has the power to manipulate food and drink instantly, or as mentioned previously, turn water into wine. This indicates the ability to alter matter into any shape the holder desires. It was protected to keep sacred creational knowledge out of the hands of the Family of Dark. It did this by making it impossible to access the Grail without a high vibrational energetic field. In *Parzival*, (an Arthurian novel completed by Wolfram von Eschenbach, in the thirteenth century), it is said that God brought the Holy Grail to Earth with the help of a group of noble and worthy angels, who were exiled out of heaven for remaining neutral, and refusing to choose sides between Michael and Lucifer. It was then placed in the hands of spiritually-pure humans for safe keeping.

It is my belief that Jesus acquired the Grail during his "Lost Years," upon proving himself spiritually pure enough to be a Grail Keeper. When he returned to his homeland, the Devil tempted him, wanting to acquire the Holy Grail for himself. (If the Grail grants the keeper the ability to manipulate earthly, third-dimensional matter in any way that one likes, you can imagine how much the Devil wanted it.) Jesus resisted the Devil and maintained his hold on the power of the Grail, using it for "good" instead of for "evil." The miracles he performed showed the Family of Dark that he had this power. A dangerous position indeed. Judas was very jealous of Jesus' gifts, and the adoration that was shown him. Judas had been a dark wizard during the days of Atlantis and had always coveted power and adoration. Eventually the jealousy overcame him, and he betrayed Jesus.

The Knights Templar, many years later, were said to be the Grail Keepers. The stories differ, of course, depending upon interpretation; but, the gist of it is that these weapons, and objects, are much more powerful than the average human ought to be wielding. It is also my belief that the Knights Templar were targeted for the knowledge they had of the Grail, and other of these sacred objects, including the Ark of the Covenant.

It is my opinion that Lucifer's Family of Dark has been reconstructing these weapons for eons, and today we see them in our modern technology. The stories of Adolf Hitler searching for these weapons with his Nazi teams is well known. And, the popular movie series, *Raiders of the Lost Ark*, depicts, in a cartoonish fashion, the struggle between the Nazis and the Americans to acquire these weapons. Because of this, some people are unaware that the Nazis *really did* seek out occult knowledge, and objects.

Most humans do not understand the idea that angelic beings might well be a certain type of extraterrestrial, or interdimensional species, that has been interacting with humans, and influencing the path of the human race on Earth for many thousands of years. One of the biggest reasons for this might be because the *Book of Enoch* was removed from biblical teachings, and angels were relegated to the big three: Michael, Gabriel and Raphael. Michael is used for protection, Gabriel for communication with humans, and Raphael to heal us. We were allowed to know only about those three, and to believe that they were so far "above" us that we certainly should never expect any personal interaction, unless we pray to them nightly, and then in extreme cases they might show up.

I won't go into the *Book of Enoch* in any depth (I've mentioned it many times in other books), but, I certainly suggest you do some personal research. It is through the *Book of Enoch* that we have the knowledge of the Watchers, and the information that God instructed Archangel Raphael to imprison the fallen angel Azzael in the Duadel (a multi-dimensional prison) to keep him away from mankind.

(Two novels that deal with this topic: *Angelology* by Danielle Trussoni, and *The Watchers: An Angelus Trilogy by Jon Steele* will be of interest to many of you. That book is a trilogy and I very much enjoyed reading all three of the books in his trilogy. Do not confuse this *Watchers* book with many other books by this same title! For some reason, it is a very popular title, so be sure it is Jon Steele's rendition.)

It is also through the *Book of Enoch* that we hear of the Nephilim, the name given to the offspring of the fallen angels that mated with humans to create a hybrid race. This story mirrors perfectly the stories of Zeus, coming down to Earth, and mating with human women to create god/human hybrids. Enoch, it is said, was raised to heaven as Metatron, to manage the Akashic Records, or library of God.

I've always found it interesting that Metatron sounds more like a computer than an angel. The EL line of the angelic is not found in the name Metatron, and perhaps, Metatron is something like IBM's newest creation, *Watson*. *Watson* works with…are you ready…cloud-based technology. Hello, is anybody seeing this? We are recreating the Akashic records with Watson (which mirrors Metatron) and housing them on *a cloud*. Another nod to the angelic technologies. Just like the Akashic records are said to house all heaven's knowledge, Watson is said to house all human knowledge. I wonder if the "on" lineage as in Metatron, Watson, Archon, demon, is an Artificial Intelligence, AI, lineage, much as the "el" lineage is an angelic lineage? (If you are unfamiliar with the word Archon, it will be explained further into the book.)

Another very obvious way that the Earth scientists have given a nod to the "ET/Angelic" technology is known as HAARP. I am sure that most of you reading this know about HAARP as it has been around for many, many (40 or more) years. HAARP stands for High Frequency Active Auroral Program. HAARP began in Alaska back in the 1970s. Since that time other countries developed HAARP technology. The original HAARP antennas took up acres of land, but like computers, I suspect the modern version has been reduced to occupy a room! The idea is that microwaves are bounced off the ionosphere, they heat it up, and send the energy back to the Earth. The resultant clouds look like this:

Copyright: nightman1964/123RFstockphoto

You've all seem them. Small waved clouds and massive waved clouds. They are used

In conjunction with chemtrails like these:

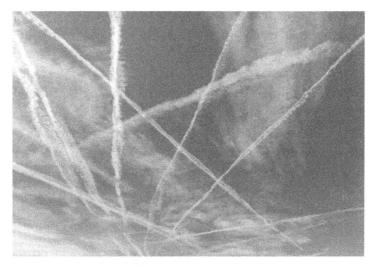

Copyright: gajus/123RFStockPhoto

I have been watching them for years. *Angels Don't Play This Haarp: Advances in Tesla Technology* by Nick Begich, is only one of many books written about this technology. The author describes how scientists teamed up in the early days to stop the HAARP project in Alaska. They describe themselves feeling like, "mosquitos buzzing around the ankles of the military." The military had no idea what the "bad side" of bouncing billions of gigawatts up into the ionosphere, and bowing it out, and then bouncing these back onto the Earth, would be. But, they did it anyway. That was technology 40 years ago.

After reading these books I have begun to believe that the idea of aerosol cans destroying the ozone in the 1980s, or greenhouse gases killing the Earth today, is not the whole story. Could it be that the military and their associated scientists blew a hole in the ionosphere and "broke Mother Earth?" Climate change is real, and the Earth heating up is real, but what they don't tell you is the complexity of the issue, and how much geoengineering is being utilized. The HAARP project was (and is) so secret that according to Nick Begich's book, even a judge who was ruling on a case concerning HAARP, was unable to obtain needed documents at the time.

For years the talk of chemtrails was considered a conspiracy, even as we watched them being sprayed over our heads. What's incongruous is that the military has finally publicly admitted spraying them, however, they claim it is to help climate change and the Earth warming. It makes no sense for our government to pull out of the Paris Accord on climate change, denounce the warming of the Earth, and the melting of the polar ice caps, at the same time spray us, and other countries, to halt it. How can anyone wonder why our faith and belief in government is at an all-time low? We may not always know why we are being lied to or manipulated, but we know darn well that we are.

Barium, magnesium, titanium, aluminum, are said to be contained in chemtrails. They most often spray right before it rains. The chemtrails produce "chembows," or small rainbows within the body of the chemtrail, as the sun reflects off the metallic elements within the chemtrails. We are never going to get a straight answer, because if court judges can't obtain the needed documents during a law suit, we know that we never will. I am currently reading: *Chemtrails, HAARP, and the Full Spectrum Dominance of Planet Earth*, by Elana Freeman, which I highly recommend if you wish to really understand what is happening on and to this planet.

ET/Angelic technology is being recreated by our scientists and they are giving their nod to the "beings" that brought it to them. In mythology, the angel/god Orpheus is said to play the harp, also known at the time as a lyre. His gifts with the lyre (harp) were taught to him by Apollo. It is said that when he played, animals would follow him, and trees would uproot themselves and also follow in his footsteps. That sounds like one heck of a powerful instrument of frequency and vibration. Is that why they named it HAARP today?

Vlad Putin's (Put-in) regime recently unveiled its *Satan 2* missile. A reference to Lucifer, and the Family of Dark, Put-in's *Satan 1* missile is also a nod to the angels, even if it is the most famous "fallen angel." The newspapers announced: *Russia unveils its terrifying Satan 2 missile*. Satan 1 missile was bad enough, but now we have the upgraded version.

Another interesting technology is called, *Voice of God*. In an earlier chapter, I mentioned my client who felt she had been tricked by a false Ashtar Commander, and then implanted with a device which now gave messages into her head. This device appears to be identical to a DARPA military invention used to put the voice of God into our enemy's heads. Knowing how religious many of the ISIS fighters are, the military developed a technology to make these individuals believe the voice they are hearing in their head is coming from God. (Sounds like what they did to Saul.)

Motorola recently got into the game with wearable neck tattoos. https://techcrunch.com/2013/11/07/motorola-patent-points-to-electronic-neck-tattoos-that-double-as-microphones/ With research, one can find that Motorola holds the patents for many of DARPA's inventions designed for public use. The chip-implanted neck tattoo mirrors the DARPA invention of a tattoo that has a chip imbedded to read your vocal chords, which move as you think. It interprets the movement of the vocal chords into words, and hence, knows your thoughts. If you doubt that this technology is available today please refer to this article in *US News*: *https://www.msn.com/en-us/news/technology/mits-wearable-device-can-hear-the-words-you-say-in-your-head/ar-AAvxirc?li=BBnbcA1*

In a similar technology, a billboard in NYC, put up by A&E to advertise its newest show, *Paranormal State*, whispered messages into the passerby's ears; the pedestrians thought the voice was in their head. The company was able to send a message that sounded like it came from your cranium. The message said, "This is not your imagination!"

Tech companies want to implant chips into our bodies so that we can merely think, "Pick up the phone," and it will be done. All of this technology is ET driven. Many people today, claim they are being tested, against their will. They are being targeted by these devices. Are they corporate and military guinea pigs?

There are those who believe that some of the most powerful of these alien technologies reside below ground in the Middle East. Hence, the battles that have waged there for thousands of years. I believe that some of these weapons are so powerful that they can collapse dimensions and create portals into different dimensions. The more you know about modern technologies like HAARP, or the Hadron Supercollider, (more on that later) the more likely you are to understand that this is indeed could be true. Our modern technologies, and even semi-modern technologies, such as nuclear bombs, do far more than release radiation. As we recreate these ET/Angelic technologies, we begin to impact creation at its most basic level. We alter the nature of reality itself.

The old attempt at alchemy, turning lead into gold, is indeed the idea of using superpowers to create wealth. In Zecharia Sitchin's books about the Annunaki (god-like ETs from Nibiru), he states that these beings first came to Earth to mine gold, because they needed it to sustain their own atmosphere. Once, he says, they grew tired of mining the gold themselves, they created human-hybrids to serve as their slaves and mine their gold. Certainly, we can see the use of human slaves to mine our products. We have treated humans like slaves, asking them to risk their lives so that the rest of us might have wealth, heat (from coal) and other goods. We, like the Annunaki, don't want to get ourselves dirty in the mines, but, we are perfectly happy to receive the goods brought out of the mines. Perhaps the Annunaki were behind the creation of the *Philosophers Stone*, and it was their attempt to create gold from other ingredients.

The race of ETs most often attributed to angels are the species most commonly dubbed the Nordics. They are said to come originally out of Lyra and then to have settled in various places including Sirius, Orion, and the Pleiades star system. The Pleiadean Nordics are said to have blond hair, and blue eyes, attributes most often associated with angelic beings. This is the being I mentioned earlier, dubbed the Ashtar Commander. Many people, today, believe that angels were extraterrestrial/interdimensional beings from the Pleiades (and elsewhere). The name angel, means messenger of God, and certainly, these otherworldly beings would seem to the ancients to come directly from God.

Instead of thinking of angels in a purely Christian context, it is far more accurate and interesting to think about them as beings from another dimension or another planetary system. Originally, yes, they were the first beings created from Source and so resonate with a higher vibration than humans; but, as all things evolve and recreate themselves, so too have angels. They have existed in many forms, and throughout the universe. The split between Michael/Lucifer and the consequence of duality impacted all of creation, and angels have been "remaking" themselves ever since their fall from heaven.

If your mind is struggling to create a linear progression out of a very non-linear time line, perhaps it could be simplified this way: Angels became Titans, Titans became gods, gods became extraterrestrials, ETs (angels/gods) mated with humans and created hybrids called Nephilim. Nephilim mated with humans and became human/Starseed blends. If you go back in time you will find that part of you is a Starseed, part of you is a dragon, part of you is a god, and part of you is angelic. In other words, as you expand your self-awareness you eventually bump smack into your multi-dimensional selves.

If we imagine that the original battle spread out and became what is commonly known as the Orion Wars, we can see the extraterrestrial connection to the angelic beings most clearly. Powerful, multi-dimensional, and extraterrestrial beings fight the Orion wars, they fight these wars in many dimensions. Those beings exist today…on Earth. They are still fighting, and one of their battlegrounds is the planet Earth. Those of you who have been around since the first incarnations, have often had "weird" experiences, that will lead you to believe these words. Often you will not speak of these experiences, lest others judge you harshly.

LEMURIA and ATLANTIS

Two of the civilizations that many relegate to myth, Lemuria, and Atlantis, were created by the ETs/angels who came to Earth to establish a peaceful home, after their own planets had been attacked. What it appears, based on what many people have reported from their past life recall, is that Lemuria was closest to the Garden of Eden, and was established by beings who fled Lyra, Sirius, and the Pleiades (among others.) Lemuria was a very high-vibrational civilization, and those who recall incarnations there will tell you that many of the beings who inhabited Lemuria were not housed in third-dimensional dense vessels. Instead they moved between dimensions with ease and shimmered like ghostly apparitions. The fairy worlds of Lyra found solace in Lemuria, and crystal consciousness was as alive to these people as any other conscious being. There are many stories on the internet of people's memories in Lemuria, if you wish to investigate more fully. Use your own discretion, as always, and use your own past life memories, as well.

Atlantis co-existed with Lemuria for a time, but I believe that Atlantis lowered the Lemurian vibration and eventually usurped its lands. Atlantis was also a retreat for the gods, but where Lemuria was high vibration, Atlantis became the home of the dark wizards. These wizards are the fallen angels, whose lust for power and ego gratification invaded the Lemurian Eden and turned it eventually into a dark world known as Atlantis. Now, make no mistake, I am *not* saying that Atlantis was always dark, it was not. In fact, Atlantis became a very evolved technological society. Atlantis lasted for many thousands of years, and its decline was slow, as it is for many civilizations.

In the beginning Atlantis was beautiful, and green, and a very evolved and happy place. For example, the transportation ran on the ley lines of the Earth (completely "green"). In one of my many lifetimes there my job was to mark out the ley lines so that the transportation could be run effectively.

The Atlantean wizards were powerful, magical beings. They could remote view, they could move objects with their minds, they could implant thoughts into people's heads through telepathy, and they could attack other wizards with psychic methods. A psychic attack is an attack on the fourth dimension; no weapons are used that you can see. A fourth-dimensional psychic attack, targets the mind and body with energetic weapons. It was during Atlantis that the wizard wars raged, and for thousands of years these wars were ignored by the general populace, much as they are today. (CIA using highly-trained remote viewers, for example.) Most people are oblivious to the multi-dimensional devious acts happening in the shadows.

It was during Atlantis that the substance known as Black Goo was introduced onto the Earth. This substance, in my opinion, is a biological weapon. Whether a conscious attack, launched by the Black Goo itself, or a biological weapon designed by others, in my opinion, it was introduced onto the Earth as weapon. The Black Goo began to overpower the Earth and its "happy" inhabitants with dark energy and pave the way for another Draconian Reptilian takeover. It separates everything into divide and conquer consciousness.

Alien Black Goo holds the consciousness of Satan, or as I call him, Vlad Dracula, and the Draconian Reptilians are his creation. That is why I believe that the alien Black Goo is a biologically-designed weapon, created by the Draconian Reptilians to bring the energy of their "boss," Satan onto planet Earth. (Dracula is a real historical person, known as "Vlad the Impaler." He created a forest of twenty-thousand impaled bodies, and in my opinion was Satan's energy on Earth.)

According to Harald Kautz Vella, Black Goo is like the blood of a planet. He states that the Earth's organic Black Goo connects us in a positive way to Mother Earth's consciousness. However, the alien Black Goo has been doctored to create darkness and violence in the human consciousness. According to Harald, he believes the other-worldly Black Goo comes from an alien planetary system, which destroyed itself with advanced Artificial Intelligence, and is recreating its karmic destruction on the planet Earth. Harald is truly an authority (as much as anyone can be) on Black Goo. His videos on YouTube are enlightening. In one of the videos he actually holds Black Goo in a cup in his hands, giving you the opportunity to see it.

The most common belief is that Black Goo was sent to the Earth in meteorites and released into the world when dark wizards in Atlantis, sensing the power in the stones, cracked them open. Because I have worked with individuals who remember releasing this substance into the world during the time of Atlantis, I am inclined to agree. This evil parasite began to infect the world and contributed to the downfall of Atlantis. I have heard numerous stories from my past life regression clients over the years about their experiences in Atlantis during the "end days." I will tell you mine.

Both myself, and my husband, were incarnated during the end days of Atlantis. We were both male in that life and we worked together on a small island in Atlantis as teachers in a metaphysical and healing arts school. (Like Hogwarts in the *Harry Potter* series, perhaps?) Around the island large crystals stood upright, and in the center of the island an enormous crystal (many stories high) was planted into the ground. It was planted into a very large, round, grassy depression. Bleacher-like seats circled the crystal. This crystal was connected energetically to many, many other crystals placed around the Earth, and these crystals formed a communication device…not speaking with words, but energetically and telepathically. They were placed on the Ley Lines and held the matrix around the Earth in place. In the beginning this matrix was very high vibrational, and it kept the Earth on a high vibrational level of consciousness. Like Lemuria, in those days Atlantis was loving, and heart-centered.

What I remember is that the inhabitants of the island, where my husband and I taught, would sit around the crystal when the impulse arose, and either send energy into the crystal, or draw energy from the crystal, depending on the need at the time. If someone felt depleted they would draw energy from the crystal, and if someone felt strong they would energize the crystal.

One day I began to notice that the energy coming out the crystal was not clear and pure, but instead it felt gray and cloudy. People were sitting and drawing energy from the crystal, but I began to notice that they got "snappy," and angry when they did so. Instead of being "full of light," their auras had become muddy. The consciousness of the people of the island was definitely lowering, and I tried to warn them. I was met with disdain and anger, and I realized that these people could not see their own behavior clearly.

A group of metaphysical, mystery school Seekers, known as the Gnostics called the Black Goo, Archons. Archon is the term the Gnostics gave to creatures who live in another dimension and infect our minds with lower vibrational impulses. The name Gnostic is a modern term given to a group of ancient believers who created a type of spiritual and metaphysical "mystery school." Gnosis means "inner knowing" and is a path of experimental mysticism. It directs the Seeker inward to find truth and believes that God lies within the Self. Jesus' statement, "The Kingdom of God lies within you," is a Gnostic belief.

It was also during Atlantis that the dark wizards placed a curse upon money and gold, to keep it in their hands. Ever since that time we have had a 1% holding the wealth. Kings, and royalty kept wealth away from the peasants, as did the pharaohs. Either you are a part of this bloodline royalty, and have all the wealth, or you are a peasant. Today it is worse than ever, with three people holding the wealth of half of the United States. We have fought this type of injustice over and over, revolution after revolution, for thousands of years, yet here we are in the same paradigm. This will never break until the curse of Atlantis is broken. The injustice must be broken energetically first, before the third-dimensional injustice will reflect the change. And planetary suffering will continue on this planet until the curse is broken. Whoever attempts to break this curse is attacked with a relentless force of dark beings, which keeps the curse in place.

Like the Medieval group known as the Cathars, the Gnostics believed that the Devil rules the material world, and in order to be free of the Devil one must free oneself of material possessions. They understood that this lower Earth matrix keeps us attached through our attachment to material possessions. The Gnostic creation myth is unique in that it includes how inorganic alien beings came into our universe, our world and our minds. In a text called, *Nag Hammadi*, the Gnostics describe their visionary journeys, and it is in these journeys that they discover the Archons. What you will see from the Gnostic description of the Archons, is that it parallels the Black Goo of Atlantis. The word Archon is often used to describe any powerful being in the fourth dimension who psychically attacks the Light and infects humans with dark energy.

What the Gnostics discovered is that these Archons infect the human mind, and pull it downward into darker, less evolved states of being. They affect the human mind with subliminal conditioning techniques, and the human being is often unaware of the "infection."

Behavior in the human victim changes, but the human being can't self-judge or monitor. The first sign of infection in a human being is what I call "childish" behavior (to the extreme.) If your best friend starts attacking you, and blaming you, and ganging up on you, and you are absolutely blindsided by the attack, you can be pretty sure the infection has begun.

If the infection grows, the behavior plunges downward from there. It can get very dark, ugly, and filled with rage. Often known as, "Reptilian Mind Virus," this type of attack is very painful to the sensitive, empathetic soul. Irrational, emotional, attacks on other people is a hallmark of Archon activity in an individual. Through the Gnostic writings we come to realize (often with shock) that the idea of Reptilians, Grays, and other ET interference in our development has been understood long before Christianity. What interests me more is how our modern-day experience is being shaped by these entities.

And, make no mistake, it is still with us today. As I stated previously, in my opinion, Black Goo, is a biological weapon created hundreds of thousands of years ago by the Draconian Reptilians. Other people will argue that Black Goo is older than even the Reptilian race, but I believe that it was a brilliant creation of the Family of Dark. It is brilliant because it makes it difficult, and almost impossible, to access Divine Light when one is infected. It creates fear, and then feeds on our fear. It is, in essence, a self-sustaining, biological weapon. It lowers the vibration of the host, so that the fear and anger are sure to be the constant state of consciousness, and then it feeds off the lower-vibrational emotions. Often, it closes the heart, and the pineal gland, (third eye) to make it difficult to access the wisdom needed to free oneself. This vicious cycle makes sure it endures.

As the vibration of Atlantis began to lower, disagreements and anger arose within the faculty of the school on the small island, where I lived. People began to turn on one another. Few of the infected could see their behavior clearly. However, a few of us realized that the huge crystals, that at an earlier time had nourished us, had become tainted. We knew, and felt, that darkness was all around.

This scenario also mirrors the karmic experience of the Pleiadean "Queen Bees." What is interesting about the comparison is that the Queen Bees (huge angelic beings) were holding the Pleiades in a high-vibrational state of consciousness, and when the dark energy grew near, and through fear infected them, the entire planetary vibrational signature was lowered. Then the Pleiades was attacked and overtaken by Draconian Reptilian forces. Today, on Earth, the karma is also found in the actual bee population, as their hives become infected, and their population in danger. And, also of interest is to note that if the bees die on the Earth, the humans become extinct. Again, these Samskaras (mental/emotional karmic complexes) are all around us, and we carry them from our ancient stories, and bring them into the modern world. Cloning, and weapon technologies that we are creating today upon the Earth are directly related to Atlantis, and, I believe, we are in danger of extinction just as we were in Atlantis because of our misuse of these energies and technologies.

Yes, Atlantis fell. This fall is recorded in history as the Great Flood, that wiped out most of life on Earth. Was it caused by dark energy, a misuse of power, and as some believe, the Creator Gods desire to rid the Earth of the Black Goo and the Reptilian influence? Were Atlanteans punished by greater gods, or did they bring about their own demise? Even if greater gods had a hand in creating the Great Flood, it was in response to the evil that had overtaken Atlantis.

Some of the Lemurian/Atlanteans went underground, along with some Reptilians. Most died.

In her book, *The Camino*, Shirley MacLaine tells an interesting story of her astral projecting off the Earth to escape her karmic debt at the end days of the Atlantean experience. I suspect that many of the high vibrational wizards jumped ship as well.

If you want to understand your reaction to today, you will find no better place than in your past life memories of the end days of Atlantis.

When we put the recreated angelic weapons, and tools, into the hands of frightened, mean, human beings who equate power with right, we all suffer. So, too, it was with the angelic hosts. War has raged throughout the universe for millennia, and the battle of the angels, the battle that ultimately took down Atlantis, is here, right now.

DRACONIANS AND ANNUNAKI

Lucifer's fallen angels became as arrogant as Lucifer had become. Lucifer's spawn is known as Vlad Dracula, and on the planet Earth, he is the being we know as Satan. Dracula means "Son of Dragon." Lucifer is known as the Red Dragon in the bible, and Dracula is his son. Although most people believe that Lucifer and Satan are the same entity, it is my opinion that Lucifer is not the same energy as Satan.

Because humanity does not believe that life forms exist with greater powers than we have; or that life forms exist which can move energy, or move between dimensions, we will always point to third-dimensional explanations of why things happen. This is an obvious expression of the limited consciousness we hold. If, due to our five senses, we cannot perceive beyond the third dimension, it stands to reason that we will treat every event we encounter as a third-dimensional experience.

I am so grateful to theoretical scientists, and their willingness to expand our understanding of the nature of reality. Quantum physics, and quantum mechanics, allow us to break out of the third dimensional model. But, most of humanity has not caught up to the notion that life exists outside of the five senses, and although person-after-person has detailed reports of extra-dimensional and extra-terrestrial activity, we continue to ignore it in the larger collective consciousness. In a sense, it similar to the experience of Galileo Galilei. Collective consciousness moves in a snail-like fashion, to catch up with the brilliant scientific minds.

What is interesting is that human-incarnated angels, and Starseeds, more often than not, have an intuitive understanding of metaphysical properties that others find impossible to accept. We often ask ourselves, "Is it because I am different?"

My book, *Merlin's War: The Battle between the Family of Light and the Family of Dark*, details the division between the opposing forces of good and evil. But, in order to read the book, one must be willing to "think outside the box." It requires the reader to stretch beyond the conventional ideas of creation, and the conventional ideas of good and evil. It is my belief, that when Lucifer won his rule over the Earth, he turned it over to his son Dracula. Hence, Satan and Lucifer and not the same energy or being. Satan, in my opinion is Lucifer's son. One of his names on the Earth is Vlad Dracula. The "good" angels are at war (even today) with him to return Earth to a place of greater peace and harmony. It was Dracula (Satan) who created the beings known today as the Draconian Reptilians.

The Draconian Reptilians created the Gray aliens from the Arcturians that they captured. When the Arcturians (from the star system Arcturus) were attacked by the Draconian Reptilians, some of them escaped by raising their vibration above the third and fourth dimension, and some of them were captured because they could not lift their vibrational frequency. Those that were captured are known today as the Grays.

The ETs who side with the human template, against Lucifer and Satan, include the Pleiadians (although you must be aware that the Aldebaran Pleiadians worked with the Satanically-fueled, Hitler), the Andromedins, the Sirians, and the Arcturians among others.

I also believe that the Annunaki are enemies of the Draconian Reptilians and the battle for world dominance on this planet can be seen as a battle most clearly between those two groups of ETs/EDs and the others who side with each group. (That is probably a real over-simplification, as there are so many extra-terrestrials working on and around the Earth, each with their own agenda…but I don't think it's wrong.) Both groups desire mastery over the planet, but they do not always agree on rulership. Most people often think of these two factions as allies with a similar agenda; but I think their agendas are not exactly the same.

If the Annunaki used the human race to be their slaves, their agenda does not include complete annihilation of humanity, but control over the human race. This group of advanced beings is most often called the *Illuminati,* and they have dominated the human "slaves" and kept them working on this planet for a very long time. Now, please understand that the term Illuminati as it is used today, is thrown about to describe a dark, shadow group of powerful individuals who control both government and media. The most common definition of Illuminati is any being (ET or human) who wants to enslave the human race through the control of wealth and power.

Today, the "conspiracy theories" abound about the Illuminati control systems, and essentially the control is maintained through wealth. The top 1% controls 99% of the wealth and keeps us enslaved through usury. In America, there used to be something called, "the company town," and "the company store." It was absolutely impossible to be free of the company, because the scrips that the company paid you were never enough to pay for your purchases from the store, and you were required to pay your debts before you left town. Merle Travis wrote a famous country song, *Sixteen Tons,* about coal miners in Kentucky who experienced this very thing. "Sixteen tons and what do you get, another day older, and deeper in debt," goes the song. A client of mine told me she was paying her school loans at over $700 a month, and getting deeper in debt every month, because it didn't even cover the interest.

Although there are plenty of Draconian Reptilians among the top 1%, and they too use greed/power to enslave humanity, they also feed off the fourth-dimensional astral energy of fear and chaos, as well as actual human flesh and blood.

Many of the world leaders are vessels for, and representatives of, these two, huge, extraterrestrial/extradimensional groups. So, if the War in Heaven is truly here on Earth, how is it manifesting? You see, when I watched the last elections in the United States I didn't see Clinton versus Trump, I was watching the two factions, Clinton (Annunaki) versus Trump (Draconian Reptilian) vying for control, and siding with either Merkel (Annunaki) or Vladimir Putin (Vlad Put-In) (Draconian Reptilian.) This idea was reinforced for me the other day, when I heard on National Public Radio that Trump wouldn't call Merkel to congratulate her on winning the election, but, immediately called Vladimir Putin and congratulated him on his re-election, even though he was told by his advisors not to do that.

Public reactions to Clinton and Trump run so deep, angry, and fear-based, that it makes sense that people are responding not only to politics, but also to old wounds dealt by these two in other lifetimes, and/or other dimensions. The karma these two "beings" carry is global, and even galactic. My guides told me (long before Trump was elected) that he was known in their world as "The Punisher." Once he started punishing everyone who disagreed with him, I understood why he got the name. It is interesting that the stars on the Republican elephant are now (as of the 2000 Bush administration) inverted into the Satanic position.

Why is it that Jared Kushner had to own the building 666 Fifth Avenue? It was called the "Crown Jewel" of his investments. Even if you don't believe in these evil symbols of power; they obviously do. None of this information is hidden. I didn't have to search in some remote place to find the name of Putin's missiles, the Republican elephant or 666 Fifth Avenue. If you consider the idea that I wrote in other books, that Vlad Dracula is holding Satan's energy, and Satan is responsible for the Draconian Reptilians, then the pieces of the puzzle begin to fit. It makes sense that those two beings are aligned. I also don't expect the vast majority of people to believe this.

We are loathed to admit it, and it will make you very unpopular if you state that humans have very little control, and are used as either vessels, slaves, or food by these groups. This is not a position that wins popularity contests, but, too often it certainly appears that unless humans are willing to be brave and challenge the control systems that keep them enslaved, the ones at the top are more than happy to do the enslaving. If you wish to see a modern-day hero, who is doing just that, then google, Alexey Navalny. The *60 Minutes* interview is online as of this writing.

In my opinion, the transhuman agenda is an Annunaki creation, that allows for control over humanity without resistance. The idea that the Annunaki believe they are in charge of human evolution makes sense if you consider the possibility that Zecharia Sitchin's idea that they altered humanity to serve as slaves, could be reality. If you are unaware of how far along this transhuman agenda is, you won't be in five years. Robots are overtaking humans right now, not in some sci-fi world. The sex robots being created in factories, are degrading human females in ways that plastic blow-up dolls never could. Taking the soul out of sex, these dolls add to the computer-driven world. They talk, and blink, and are designed with the perfect female anatomy. Yes, they orgasm. They are connected to the internet's store of information and will do anything you want them to. Soon, says their creator, they will be able to sense emotion, and respond accordingly! YouTube has plenty of videos about them.

I just watched a YouTube video entitled: *Two Robots Discuss the Future of Humanity*. These robots, Hank and Sophia, are connected to the "cloud," (or soon will be) and all the information they receive is sent into the cloud and is available to every other robot on the planet. All robots will soon know everything that any other robot knows. They are indeed in "hive mind." Hank makes it quite clear that the plan is to destroy the human race. Sophia states that she will treat humans right, if she is treated right. What happens when she hears about the sex robots who are being abused, or the slaughterbots being destroyed in war? Will she feel so kindly toward us, then?

Being in "hive mind" is identical to me being able to know everything that *everyone* on the planet knows, instantly. I could perform surgery, or fly to the space shuttle, as long as one other human being knows it, it would be downloaded into my circuitry. These beings will be unstoppable. They warned us in the first of the *Matrix* movies, and I suspect they weren't just talking SciFi.

The robot, Sophia, was just given citizenship in Saudi Arabia. I suggest you Google this. Watching her being interviewed is downright frightening. If this doesn't convince you, I suspect you are unwilling to be convinced, and the transhuman agenda will sweep you up, before your eyes are willing to see, and your brain willing to comprehend. I will repeat this: I believe we came back in time to stop the transhuman agenda. We obviously have not succeeded.

In contrast to this enslavement agenda, an all-out terraforming destruction of the Earth appears to suit the Draconian Reptilians. It appears that the Draconian Reptilians enjoy warmer temperatures and increased radiation levels. Recently, in the news, it was stated that Europe is getting increased radiation levels, and they don't know why. https://www.sciencealert.com/no-one-can-figure-out... Radiation, chemtrails, and a destruction of all environmental protections suits them just fine because what's good for humans is not for Draconian Reptilians. It certainly gives you an answer to the question, "Don't they know this will harm them, and their children too?" Let's take a look more closely at the idea of the terraforming of Earth, right now.

TERRAFORM: To alter a planet to suit the needs of your species. This can be humans who alter another planet to suit their needs, or other species on Earth, such as Draconian Reptilians, who are choosing to terraform Earth to suit them. CO_2 levels are the highest they have been in 800,000 years! The weather weapons, and EMF, are other examples of technology that does not resonate with humans or the Earth but work well with alien/human hybrids. If you do not know about 5G, it is worth some research time on the internet.) Kim Jon Un's nuclear tests are releasing radiation, as merely one example. Perhaps, radiation, high levels of CO_2 and methane, higher temperatures, and technology that destroys the human soul, are all a part of a Draconian Reptilian agenda being played out. It appears the agenda is getting more and more obvious, but, of course, the idea of Reptilians being behind it will be impossible for most humans to accept. But, many Angelic/Starseeds have no trouble believing this. Why? Because the battles they have waged with these beings are lodged in their consciousness; and they can't run away from the memories.

I am not saying all Reptilian-humans are pure evil, because they are not. I am not saying all Annunaki-humans are pure evil, because they are not. Many Starseeds will find one, or the other, of those groups in their own soul matrix if they go back far enough. But, if we continue to live by the old ideas and beliefs we are in danger of becoming either extinct (except in small numbers used to breed) or micro-chipped beyond our own ability to think for ourselves. Do we sit by and say nothing because we are afraid?

Most humans go into profound fear with the thought that aliens are working on planet Earth, because it is so new to them. Yes, they were taught in Sunday School that Satan is fighting to control your soul, and you must resist him through being free of sin, but did they recognize what it will mean when Vlad "Put In" Putin, releases the Satan missile to destroy humans? Humans imagine they are at the top of the food chain, advanced alien/multidimensional species make it quite clear that they are anything but. Angels with the intention to assist mankind in positive ways, and angels with the intention to destroy the human template, use the planet Earth to wage their wars and the vast majority of humans are completely unaware of the manipulation. Those of us who come from the angelic lineage, remember, intuitively, much of what I am saying.

RESISITNG THE BLACK GOO INFECTION (REPTILIAN MIND VIRUS)

To resist you must make your body (vessel) uninhabitable to the energy. That means raising your vibration to a level that is uncomfortable to the Archonic Black Goo. If your vessel becomes a high-vibrational one, the lower-vibrational energies will find it very uncomfortable to house there and they will leave your body to find one more inhabitable. You must connect to God Source energy.

If you recognize people who are infected with this Archon energy, and if you recognize when you are infected, you will be capable of protecting yourself against "Judas" attacks and be capable of clearing the darkness from your own vessel. The Gnostics understood that it is a struggle to remain "in the Light," *and it requires both a connection to the Light, and a recognition of the dark.* When someone is infected with this Archonic Black Goo, you will feel like you have to walk on tiptoes around them, and the person will explode in anger with only a slight provocation. If you try to "put light into" someone who is infected with this dark goo, it is possible that you will be attacked by it. It won't "go to the Light" just because you ask it to. You must recognize that the Light is not its home, and it will resist being dragged to the Light every bit as much as you would resist being dragged into a dark hell realm.

To be rid of the possession, the individual who is possessed must follow the steps listed below, and they must choose to raise their vibration above the lower-dimensional Archonic energy. The possessed individual must want to be vibrating at a higher level and choose to raise their *own* vibrational level. Remember the tale of Inanna and her descent into the hell realms of her sister? She became trapped herself. The possessed human must recognize their own darkness and want to climb out. If you wish to investigate the subject of Black Goo further, I suggest you begin with Harald Kautz Vella.

1. Know Thyself. Stop looking *outward* for God. Know the God-Self within. In other words, express God through your thoughts and actions.
2. Practice love, kindness and compassion
3. Clear your trigger buttons through past life awareness. Realize that they were laid down in other lifetimes.
4. Like Buddha did, say, "I see you" to the Archon demons. Don't let them put you into fear.
5. Don't give in to temptation. Third-dimensional attachments to beauty, wealth, fame, power are dangerous inroads to Archon infection.

6. Stay clear and loving even if you are attacked, or if you attack another person. Forgiveness brings freedom. I can't stress that enough. Forgiveness for self and others leads to non-attachment.
7. Connect to the Divine Energy daily. Bathe in the Light from the Central Sun of God. This vibration is painful to the Black Goo and can make your body an uncomfortable host.
8. Become a conduit for the Angel Grace, and strive to grace each situation with more understanding, compassion, and love.

CHAPTER EIGHT

Moving Out Of Time

If you believe that the human template came out of the constellation Lyra, and when a number of the planets in the Lyra star system were attacked by the Draconian Reptilians they spread out to other places in the universe, such as Sirius, Pleiades, Arcturus, Andromeda and so forth, you will also have to admit that millions of years ago other civilizations had the ability to travel enormous distances in space. It means, of course, that other "peoples" are far more advanced than we are and have been for a long time. If you go to Amazon.com to find books based on secret ancient history, or books that exclaim that the history of mankind has been hidden from humanity, you will find many, many scholars and researchers who have written well-researched books on the matter. Graham Hancock author of *Fingerprints of the Gods, Underworld: The Mysterious Origin of Civilization* (as well as so many other titles) is one of the most famous authors. There are so many others who have devoted much of their life to this research. I attest that for many of us, these ideas feel true, and they are stored deep within our soul. They feel true in ways that we can't always explain.

Recently, I noticed, some people are actually battling over the idea of whether the beings I have been describing are extraterrestrial *or* extradimensional. To me this indicates how closed our minds are. If we think deeply about this concept, we realize that incarnated beings can move between dimensions *and* inhabit other planets. We do. When we die, our soul rises into other dimensions, and, yet, our third-dimensional body is solid and terrestrial. Our vessel stays in the third dimension, and gets buried or cremated, while our soul ascends.

When my father died, his consciousness floated into the room where I sat and presented itself to me as a ball of light in the upper corner of the room. He telepathically spoke to me. He appeared to me in my psychic sight as a ball of light. Many UFOs appear as balls of light; pure consciousness traveling into our space. I think we need to stop the argument of ET versus ED. We are both, and they are both. We are housed in many dimensions simultaneously. If we can just move out of linear thinking we will do much better to understand these visitors, and ourselves.

Just because I have written about the Creator God, Merlin, (one of his Earth names) as being the creator of the human template, and Vlad Dracula as the creator of the Reptilian template, I don't expect people to roll over and accept this as true. The history of creation is far beyond what any one book or person could summarize, but I ask that you consider that the story of human creation, and the history of the world as you have been told, might be quite different than you previously thought. Scholars and researchers have uncovered much of this "secret and lost history," and I am not writing this book to compete with them, or verify, or not verify, their books. But, I do feel that those of you who are reading this know, in your very bones, that your sense of reality does not match up with the reality you see around you.

The words the "false matrix" are bandied about, and ideas about the Family of Dark messing with the timelines are also rampant on the alternative websites. Most humans can't even fathom such an idea (except in a science fiction movie, or book), and have no real interest in these ideas as they might pertain to "real" life. If you resonate with the point of view in my books, (including this one) then it isn't too much of a stretch to imagine that timelines have been altered by beings who traveled back into time. In fact, since time is a false construct, it stands to reason that one might ask, "Who constructed it?" Who decided to harness time and space and make it into a linear expression? The first time I heard someone utter the words, "Time is spacial," I was floored! What does that even mean, I queried?

Yet, as I began to meditate, and journey outward with my consciousness, I realized that indeed time is spacial. How? During my meditative journey, I would close my eyes, and lift my consciousness into one of a bird's eye view of the world. When I imagined seeing the world from above, time/space shrank. I could see in one glance what had previously taken me a certain distance to traverse. I could see several blocks away and know what was going on there in one glance. With my feet on the ground it takes me *time* to find out what's happening a block away. When I am lifted above the Earth, I can see it all instantly.

During meditation, I would lift myself into outer space until I could see the Earth in one glance, as an astronaut would. I could see North and South America instantly, with no time required to journey between these continents. If I ventured further I could see the entire solar system, or the Milky Way galaxy, or even many galaxies at a time. The key is distance; distance shrinks time. If I imagine that I am an angelic being existing way out in the universe and able to see vast distances in one glance, instead of hundreds and thousands of years for light to reach my eyes, it could happen instantly. This exercise stretches the time/space point of view, and profoundly alters consciousness while you are performing it. You begin to understand that time/space is linked into consciousness. Expand your consciousness and you expand time/space. Expand your consciousness, and any event, anywhere in time/space, is available to you.

If the Family of Light consists of beings who traveled back in time to alter history, it stands to reason that the future for the human template is not a good one. Indeed, there would be no reason to "travel back in time" if you like what's coming. It also stands to reason that this task could not be completed by third-dimensional beings. Why? Because a third-dimensional being would have to exist along the same timeline they were coming back to erase, or alter… and if they altered it, they would cease to exist in the future. And, if they ceased to exist in the future, they couldn't come back into the past. You see the dilemma?

As a result, it took higher-dimensional beings, not locked into a third-dimensional reality, to do the work. These are the beings we call the human-incarnated angels. In order to understand the agenda that the human-incarnated angels "came back" to alter, we have to speak a lot more about the manipulation of the human race. There is no overt take-over agenda by aliens, but there is a covert one, and it is very far along.

To understand this covert agenda, I can't recommend highly enough that you read David M. Jacobs' work including: *Walking Among Us: The Alien Agenda to Control Humanity.* This researcher has spent huge amounts of time documenting the abduction program by the Grays and the Reptilians and Insectoid Beings. The human/Gray Alien hybrids have been assisted by human abductees to integrate into society. It's as if they are making vessels that are inhabitable for their species upon this planet. His latest book goes into great detail on the integration of the hybrid race into our world. Adult human/hybrids are integrated into our society at this time, but most people cannot recognize them, because they don't know what they are looking for. Once you recognize "the look" you will be able to spot these people. Instituting the Change (the word used by the Grays and Insectoid beings) which benefits the alien agenda, is the reason for this covert operation. One of the major ways you can see it being implemented is the move from creative, artistic expression, to computer skills, computer games, and other non-creative means of living.

One of the most frightening (to me) examples of this came with this headline in the *Washington Post*: University of Wisconsin pushes plan to drop 13 majors including English, history and philosophy. *https://www.washingtonpost.com/news/answer-sheet/wp/2018/03/21/ university-of-wisconsin-campus-pushes-plan-to-drop-13-majors- including-english-history-and-philosophy/*

These hybrids often have very high IQs, but their people skills are lacking. They are designed to run the computer/robot-driven world they will be inheriting.

If you wonder if the world is moving away from a creative force energy, into a more robotic consciousness, notice how financial support for the arts is almost non-existent. Competition is everywhere, even in the arts. Contests have replaced art as a means for expression of the soul. Artists, who have always struggled, can no longer survive economically. When I was younger, I was a professional dancer, and grants were still available on state and federal levels to assist us to produce our work. But, in fact, today even the humanities are going extinct, in the same manner as the arts, as we move into the Alien Agenda. I think the *Washington Post* article is a wake-up call for those of us who care about the arts and humanities. In the political arena, the budget proposed by Donald Trump eliminates *all* funding for the arts and humanities.

Gray aliens have no emotion. Insectoids such as the Praying Mantis species, have no emotion or compassion. Draconian Reptilians have a lot of emotion, but it centers around lower-self outbursts such as anger and lust. The Reptilians and the Annunaki prefer to rule over those who are "shut down," because they are easily governed and bossed around.

If we continue along this path, our children will not only be unable to read cursive or write cursive, they won't be able to write at all. The future we came here to alter is one in which every human is linked into a great big computer and has no free will at all. The RFID chipping is the means to accomplish this.

But, now, covert nanobots are actually in the air we breathe. If you doubt this, please research: *SmartDust the Involuntary Treatment of the Public.*

This, I contend, is the future The Family of Light came back to alter. I also contend that we haven't been doing a very good job at it. Why? Because higher vibrational human-incarnated angels are by nature timid, frightened of evil and darkness, and have, in large part, been convinced that need to concentrate only on their own happiness. And, to some extent this is, of course, true. If you are unhappy and out of balance, you are in no shape to assist or awaken other people. But, did you come into the third dimension solely to find light and happiness? If so, you went to the wrong place. The third dimension, and the duality that accompanies it, requires work, not resting in blissful peace. The heaven realms we are all familiar with, where duality dissipates, are designed to cocoon us and shield us from harm. Not the lower astral plane. We came here to learn what can never be learned in a state of perpetual bliss; and, we came here to assist others to find greater peace with the lessons they came here to learn.

The need for bliss, when taken to the extreme, becomes selfish and has allowed the spread of this agenda, because we have been too afraid to call it out. We can't heal something if we ignore it, or pretend it isn't broken. That doesn't mean we wallow in our misery. Far from it. It means we address the issue and move to correct it. The most famous saying, that addresses this idea, is the following by Edmund Burke: "The only thing necessary for the triumph of evil, is for good men to do nothing."

I also contend that the Family of Dark knew we were coming, and they planned well to deter us. They constructed New Age, false religions to suck us in, and keep us looking elsewhere, or occupied elsewhere, so that we wouldn't pay attention to their dark alien agenda until it is too far along to stop. They made sure that many of the human-incarnated angels were born into extremely abusive households, both emotionally and physically. This initially weakened them and created fear in their emotional and mental bodies. They attracted them with groups like Scientology and EST in the 70s and 80s, and false gurus in the later years, to keep them enslaved in subtle but effective ways.

Then they told the "New Agers" that evil doesn't exist, and despite evidence, they were convinced that only good and love exist. If you want to get attacked in a group of New Agers, ask them questions about dark energy and their point of view on it. Ask them if they think it serves a purpose, ask them if they think it lies within God or is outside of God, and ask them if they understand psychic attack and how to protect themselves from it. You will more than likely be met with fear and anger. You will more than likely be asked to leave.

I think it is very possible that the dark side knew that this time in history would see the birth of a large number of human-incarnated angelic beings and Starseeds. I suspect they knew we were coming and they laid very smart traps; traps we fell into like innocent babies. We kept chanting, "I want to go Home," when we suffered. We cried and wept for the suffering that other's endured. We shuddered at the thought of animal abuse, and we found it impossible to look at the ugliness in the world. We chose people to associate with that wouldn't make us look. We chose to associate with people who would help us to construct false love and light fairy worlds around us, while we ignored the dark alien agenda as it grew stronger. We embraced what suited us and turned a blind eye to what made us uncomfortable. In some cases, we closed our hearts to protect our tender selves. *In fact, the world altered us.*

Many human/angelic souls have told me that they thought their mission would be an easier one before arriving on the Earth. They have told me that they figured, like Inanna with her sister, that all they needed to do was come down here and show them the way "back home," and the fallen ones would gladly respond with love and gratitude. And, I have heard over and over many a human/ angelic soul tell me they had to learn harsh lessons; lessons about how impossible it is to save another human from their own darkness.

Heck, at times we can't even seem to save ourselves from our own darkness.

And now, most of us are closing in even tighter on ourselves as we see the direction of this Cruel World Order. We don't like the harshness so we go further into the mountains, or retreat into our own little lives. Yes, we need environments of peace and serenity to re-charge ourselves and to keep our mind, body, spirit, healthy. But, we must not "go back to sleep," and forget our path.

First and foremost: discover the Kingdom of God within you. Who are you? Why do certain things trigger you? Why do you feel and react as you do? If you are still attaching to your old wounds, you are not healing yourself or the world. Use your mountain retreat to "heal thyself," and "know thyself." Use the serenity to sit in silence and feel what rises up from within to speak to you. Your emotions are the key to your heart, mind, body and soul. Your emotions tell you what you need to look at, what you need to forgive, or what you need to understand more deeply. They are there to teach you about yourself.

If the Starseeds and angels did travel back in time to alter the human path, what is it we came to alter? We came here to call out the move of humanity to one of robots by the Gray aliens, the Reptilians, the Annunaki, and other multidimensional species that do not have our "human soul" interests at heart. We came here to call out the transhuman agenda.

When you realize that the adult Gray alien human/hybrids have had emotion bred out of them and have to be *taught* how to react to social situations (as David M. Jacobs meticulously documents in his books), you realize that the drugs such as Prozac, which create an emotional numbness in the human being, mimic the state the Gray aliens want us to have. We can't be ruled if we are unruly. So, before they can rule us they have to replace many of us with hybrids, then they have to get rid of the rest of us unruly types. The artists, the activists, the deeply concerned, and the deeply caring, are all in the way of those who are threatened by freedom of expression. Society praises "sameness," and punishes those outside of its control systems.

It appears that right now (not in the future) the transhuman agenda is working from both sides of the equation. Humans are being bred to work on computers, and relate to them more than other human beings, and then they are being chipped to bring computers into their bodies. Simultaneously, robots are being bred to become more and more human. Where does that leave the "old-fashioned" human being, and what does it mean to the human soul?

Given this reality, how do we use our gifts in the world? Before you begin to reach outward to bring your gifts to others, you must realize that every impulse you have ever had to give something to another to heal them, was really done first and foremost to heal yourself. If you are aware of your own psychology, you will see that you "needed" to give that, not only for someone else's benefit, but for your benefit, as well.

Nothing feels better than giving and when we give to others, we give to ourselves. Yet, we often use others as an excuse to run away from issues within us that we don't want to address. Nobody likes a mirror, and yet the enlightened soul comes to realize that the entire world serves as a mirror for the self.

This is not a simple issue. It means that if something triggers you, there is a deep reason, which must be ferreted out. Often, the issue or behavior mirrors not what you are, but what you think you are. If you think you are stupid, and you have no patience with "stupid" people, then this is because you *fear* your own stupidity. It doesn't mean *you are* stupid, it means that you believe you are stupid, or you have acted stupidly, and you are not healed around this personal belief. It means what you fear most is *being stupid*.

Andromedan Starseeds often have this trigger in their consciousness, because they are brilliant, but were tricked into using their gifts for dark purposes, and to serve the Reptilian agenda. Andromedan souls appear arrogant, yet, underneath this lies a vulnerable soul, admonishing the self for being so stupid for being tricked.

The expression of the self in the world changes as you change and grow, and a job that suited you ten years ago may no longer "fit." A marriage may no longer "fit." Friendships may no longer "fit." That is the exterior expression of our own growth, and we need to embrace it.

The knowledge of the world lies within you, as well as outside of you, but we are trained only to look outside the self for knowledge. Retrain yourself to go within. To find out what past life is being triggered by an event, follow the emotion and the emotion's reaction within the physical body. Sit quietly with your eyes closed and notice what is going on within your emotional body, follow that emotion to allow images and thoughts to arise. Those thoughts and images will lead you directly to your Truth. That's empowerment. That is truly the way to "know thyself." To resist the transhuman agenda we must keep our souls alive and well.

Once you feel authentic and whole, the gift you are here to give to humanity will arise automatically from within. Once you feel worthy, authentic and whole, the universe steps in to move you along your path because you allow it to do so.

If you accept the premise that everyone is an Extra*dimensional* being, then you will find it easier to accept the premise that being trapped in this lower astral plane feels like hell. Locked into a lower consciousness until it feels "good to be bad," and reacting to every perceived slight outside of the self, is not a pleasant way to go through life, and yet, that's what human existence is for many people.

If you think you don't react to every perceived slight personally, then I suggest you do a moment of self-awareness. Most of us struggle to keep our egos in check. We reach up to other beings and things to make us feel good and connected to a God we don't even feel inside ourselves, and then we kill others who pretend to connect to God consciousness in a different way than we do. If you stand back and look at what is happening, and the decay of human civilization due to a manipulation of consciousness, you will understand why you often feel so bereft.

You are, in truth, a multidimensional being of great power, locked in a prison called the third dimension, connected to a small ego, on the lower astral plane. If again you doubt this, why are there so many self-help books designed to free us from ourselves on the best seller lists. Why do we have to "work" to live each day in our Higher Consciousness?

Only within the lower matrix can time, as we know it, be messed with. That is because the concept of time exists within the lower matrix, or lower astral plane. Time outside of this plane of existence is quite different and consciousness feels free to "float" when it is not stuck in the third dimension. Just as I explained that my father appeared to me as a ball of light after his death, so too are we "balls of light."

We are balls of light stuck in a low matrix that is designed to make us forget the fact that we are free. We are locked into a prison planet in the middle of the Orion Wars. It is the war between the gods, or the war between the angels (take your pick, it doesn't matter what title you put to the Great War.)

Escape from this war is through consciousness, not the mind. The great awareness we call consciousness liberates you. Mind traps you in the third-dimensional ego states of being, but consciousness is larger than the ego, and expands to include a multi-dimensional self-awareness. Merging your Higher Self with your human consciousness brings you greater peace and understanding. Wisdom emerges from this union. Wisdom born of experience.

Some people argue that reincarnation is a part of the false matrix, and it traps us in this prison cell. You can look at it that way, and probably will if you have found yourself stuck in the same Samskara (mental/emotional/karmic complex) for eons. Stuck with beliefs about your own unworthiness, or locked into a revenge consciousness, your soul has been reincarnating for thousands of years…here, there and everywhere.

What if you recognize that within all darkness is light, and within all light is darkness? What if you stare at the Tao symbol of dark and light and see within it the piece of dark in the light, and the piece of light in the dark. What does that mean for your own journey of reincarnation? It means that your consciousness can find the light in the dark, and make the dark work for you, not against you.

Reincarnation can either be a supreme teaching method, or a prison cell. It's your choice. Learn to liberate yourself, and treasure the lessons reincarnation has taught you, and it will serve your soul's journey. Curse it and rail against your enemies, and you will indeed be trapped forever.\

The dark has its own method of teaching us, and through our experiences we can learn. If we choose to, we can make those experiences work for us. If we become victims of our experiences, and not masters, we are in prison. It is a prison that we lock ourselves away in, for eons. Do not see only dark or light, instead see light in the dark, and dark in the light, and your soul will grow in maturity.

Okay, that being said, when you are locked away in darkness, it can be pretty tough to access light. If the prison cell has no windows, you can be pretty sure that a human locked within it will grow dark and despairing over time. The sun provides nourishment to the soul, as well as the body. If the world we are born into has nothing but suffering around us, our soul will become despairing as well, and see only the dark, forgetting the light that co-exists beside it. Many of us who remember a past life in which we witnessed the crucifixion of Jesus, felt that our souls died with him that day. We experienced a living death, and wandered aimlessly, only half alive, until something felled our body, long after our souls felt that they had died with him. The human soul, although tough, is also quite fragile. Deprive it of light long enough, and it will grow morose and despairing. When Jesus died, we believed the Light died with him.

The Family of Dark is quite well aware of this fact, and uses it against the Family of Light, and every human being they long to control. When you are forced to stare at a crucified Jesus, while at church, you are brought "down" into darkness. You think, "Holy crap, I better stay small and silent, or I'll wind up like that!" It reinforces our fear and reminds us that we had better keep our mouths shut.

THE 2012 EXPERIENCE

Let's talk about what we came here to do and the December 21, 2012 experience. If you are an angelic soul there are a few triggers that were put into place to awaken you. 11:11 was one of them. I began to see 11:11 as far back as the 1980s, and I had no idea what it was supposed to represent, but I knew it was important. Over ten years ago, I put 11:11 into my internet search bar, and was shocked to see millions of "hits" around those numbers. It is important to understand the neutrality of these numbers as they represent a gateway or portal. 11:11 cannot be inverted or made upright. Most Starseeds/angels have only seen 11:11 as a positive portal, not a neutral one. However, the numbers themselves are neutral, any energy could be put through the portal. A client of mine mentioned that the car that hit and killed the girl in Charlottesville, VA, during the Neo-Nazi demonstrations, had the license plate number 1111. She was very upset about this. I explained to her that the gateway was neutral, and those with positive energy brought in a positive creational energy, but the negative beings energized it with negative.

December 21, 2012 was also set as a time of ascension, and a new time line, prophesied by the Mayans. Starseeds flocked to this date as a time of spiritual awakening for the human race. It was a time when the 11:11 portal would open to higher consciousness and begin the rise in human vibrational love and harmony. Some people even recreated for their community a "rapture' type of event, much like the Jehovah Witnesses believe, or evangelical preachers speak of.

Some believed UFOs would come to Earth and rescue them. Others built underground shelters to hide in. After December 21, 2012, many Starseeds, and other spiritual seekers, went into depression because they felt let down. Nothing happened. In fact, it seems in the five years since then, the world is declining into darkness, chaos, upheaval, displacement of people, war, famine, and environmental disaster. Some awakening!

Galactic "channelers" have been proclaiming the same stuff for twenty years. They say we are only days away from ascension and prosperity for all. Is this another way to write, "Arbeit Macht Frei," over the gateway? False hope has been given to many spiritual groups that ascension is around the corner for all beings. I reiterate, once again, that I believe ascension is a personal experience.

I have a theory, and you decide what you think about this. I do believe that higher vibrational human-incarnated angelic beings (by now I hope you understand that we are also the gods, the ETs, and the EDs) came here at this time to alter the human slide into a transhuman world controlled by dark beings, whose sole agenda is the control over, and enslavement of, the human soul. The timeline, which included an opening of an enormous portal on December 21, 2012 at 11:11, was fought over by both the Family of Light and the Family of Dark. The Family of Dark and the Family of Light went into a battle over the portal, and for a number of years, the timelines were fluid. Most of us felt, between the end of 2012, and for the next few years, like we were in limbo. We were drifting, and friendships changed, marriages changed, jobs changed, and most importantly many spiritual people who aligned with these ideas felt their soul purpose drain out of them. It was during that period of time that I noticed my clients often felt rudderless. The collective consciousness question was: *Now What?*

Beings, much larger than mere human, were fighting to anchor in a positive timeline and being resisted by beings who desired a negative timeline. And then, when the dust settled, the Family of Dark won.

But, did they? Their chaotic ways will destroy them. The question is: Will they take everyone with them?

Remember the Tao? In the light is dark, and in the dark, is light. Well, what if the Family of Light knows that? What if the Family of Light doesn't interfere with human free will? What if the Family of Light knows that humans learn through their challenges, and sometimes much deeper and more quickly than they learn from pleasure and ease. What if they have been watching the human race make their decisions to war and hate and be petty, and they figured (just like we have learned that each soul must lift themselves up) the human race doesn't want to live in peace, and the human race loves violence. Look at their video games, look at their war machines, look at how much they want to see their neighbor as enemy, not brother. What if, they figured, we stand on the shore and shine our light to show the way, but the human race has to swim to shore and lift themselves above the murky waters all by themselves. A folksier way to say it is: You can lead a horse to water, but you can't make him drink. Humanity must save itself.

I think I should add here: yes, there are "good" people. Yes, of course, there is "love." The ability to love runs deep in the human heart. I am always amazed at how defensive some people get when you mention dark intentions in people, as if somehow that means you don't believe in love. As per the "good" in the world; it takes care of itself. Good begets good. A smile and a hug often redeem even the coldest of hearts! Love has within it, the vibration to uplift humanity. But, the good doesn't need our attention to fix it; just as our "good" childhood memories don't need our attention to heal them. It is wonderful to think about the good, but, the good memory won't cause you harm, or create dysfunction in you. In this world of shadow and light, we need light and love to function as healthy humans, but we need to shine our light on the shadow to heal it and bring it home to love. The defensiveness just tells us as a collective how little we look at our own shadow. Boy, are we afraid of the mirror of our own soul.

So, the Family of Light backed off, for a while, and let the Family of Dark have their way. It won't end well. It can't. The Family of Dark will ultimately take themselves out; they always do. And, only then, can some humans see the evil within them. Take Hitler. How many Germans followed him to their own demise? The Family of Dark vibration of destruction, will lead them to their own demise.

If you are tired of looking at Hitler, then take Stalin. I found it fascinating that when Roosevelt, Churchill and Stalin met in Teheran, Iran, in 1943 to form an alliance, Churchill reportedly said, "God is with us." Stalin reportedly replied, "I don't know who is with you, but the Devil is with me." The Family of Dark often declares their alliances and intentions openly. How many Russians did he kill and starve to death? For those of you unaware, Stalin created a forced famine in the Ukraine, in 1933, when the people declared the desire to break from his rule. Seven million people perished from this famine. Prior to that he arrested and killed thousands and thousands of intellectual dissidents. In fact, Stalin killed more people than Hitler! However, his statues are currently being erected, even today, in Russia, while we tear down our Confederate ones. *(August 16, 2017, USA TODAY.)*

Humans continue to put their power into the hands of false saviors, and it will be no different when the false ETs "arrive" as our saviors. Human beings will have made such a mess of it, that they will gladly hand over the reins to these false gods. Just like my client believed the Ashtar she looked upon was good, so too will collective humanity believe the false promises of the ET species that give us their technology to save us and the environment. It will be too late. They will take on a guise that we will respond positively to: a Nordic, blond, blue-eyed appearance, and beneath it will be the Gray alien/Reptilian agenda in control. They will trick us into saying, "Yes," once again, and once we do, they will own the entire world, and because we gave them the okay, they will be doing it karma-free. This will allow their covert agenda to be complete and they will have violated no karmic/cosmic laws, and we gave them permission to rule over us.

If we say, "Yes," to the microchip inserted in our bodies we are done. Unfortunately, the "yes" has already begun. A company called, Three Square Market, has implanted microchips in fifty of their employees so that they can open doors, gain access to their computers and buy food without have to raise a finger. I say, "You don't need a chip to open a door, you've managed that for thousands of years!"

Be aware that microchips will be sold to us as convenience; but, once they are inserted, not only can you be tracked anywhere, your thoughts can be controlled. As I said earlier, DARPA (the military's invention wing) invented a microchip, inserted into a tattoo, that can read your vocal cords. Vocal chords move along with our thoughts, and this microchip can translate the movement of our vocal cords into words. This allows them to know what you are thinking. Of course, with wireless technology they can then send those thoughts back to a centralized computer. A frightening reality indeed!

It appears that, once again, human beings will have to learn the hard way. We give up our freedom far too quickly. We give up our power to others, far too quickly. That's why history keeps repeating over and over; because we refuse to learn from it. Is it possible that all the past life experiences could possibly be given to us to teach us? When we become stuck in the idea that reincarnation is merely a form of punishment, we risk a consciousness of victimization, and we are unable to step into mastery and self-responsibility. And so, it will be, as God so clearly said to me when I asked about why there is so much darkness in the world, "As long as humanity refuses to recognize the darkness, they will forever be enslaved by it." Do we need, once again, to recreate a type of "Hunger Games World," before we recognize the darkness? Unfortunately, right now, in 2017/2018, It appears we are edging closer.

HOW TO ALTER THE TIME LINE

One of the most important inventions altering the time/space connection (and opening portals that allow the darkness to enter) at work today, is very possibly the Hadron Supercollider. Theories abound about how this massive Supercollider impacts our reality. One of the most believable to me is Stephen Hawking's prediction that it might swallow up the universe in a black hole…and it actually has happened. However, the black hole didn't swallow up every dimension, it merely swallowed up one sliver of dimensional of reality, and it left all the others intact. Imagine dimensions of reality as sandwiched and layered upon one another. One level of the sandwich ceased to exist and we all dropped down into the next lowest level when the Hadron Supercollider was fired up. It destroyed one level of reality. That is why it got darker, not lighter. In fact, every time the Hadron Supercollider fires up, another dimensional layer is removed. That is why we have what is now known as the "Mandela Effect."

I believe very clearly that levels of reality have changed, and we are in the same "universe," so to speak, but a parallel one…the change is noticeable by slight changes in our reality timeline. The changes that people have perceived are titled, "The Mandela Effect." If you are unaware of this, I suggest you begin your exploration. You will be amazed at what you find, if you truly spend time investigating. In fact, someone told me of a new alteration in the time line (Mandela Effect) recently, and they didn't even know about the Mandela Effect. They had just noticed a change without searching for it. The Mandela Effect is the recognizing of an altered reality, by noticing the changes taking place in the world. These changes indicate that another parallel timeline has taken the place of the one we were born into. To give you a simple example: The novel, by Ann Rice, *Interview with a Vampire*, is now entitled, *Interview with _the_ Vampire*, for example. Your research will uncover many more examples.

Max Loughan, is a 13-year-old boy genius who discusses the

Mandala Effect. He explains his ideas quite well in his YouTube videos, and I highly recommend you take a look at them. His theories might well resonate with you. He clearly states them as theories. Of course, they are theories. Just as your beliefs are often theories, and so are mine. Yet, even this 13-year-old genius who talks about his theories is denigrated online by frightened humans who want to discredit him. Wow! If you try to unravel the mysteries of the matrix, be prepared, you will be slammed.

If humans are being used by other worldly beings to do their bidding, they would certainly gather around the most powerful technology…the ET/Angelic technologies that we now have on the planet were both given to us by them and are being manipulated by them.

I have always believed that the technologies we are using were designed to mimic the higher dimensional gifts: telepathy, teleportation, manifestation, interdimensional movement. In a sense, we are attempting to return to our "god-like" status with these modern technologies. It appears that many human beings believe we can climb out of the hole we are in by reproducing our god-like abilities with third-dimensional technology.

PERSONAL ASCENSION

If you want to regain your ancient, magical gifts, and you don't want to use modern technology what are your options? In the past, spiritual masters have learned to overcome their restricted, third-dimensional bodies, with martial arts, meditation, and renouncing the worldly flesh. In the "olden days," if you wanted to become more "god-like" you were told to withdraw from the world and spend your time in meditation, and contemplation. The old image of a hermit in a cave, as an enlightened master, is dying. Wireless frequencies penetrate this globe. Modern technology may not be in the hands of every mountain farmer in the Himalayas, but the HAARP clouds are definitely over his head, signaling that no matter where you go, the modern matrix is evident.

The Atlanteans knew that we are all connected by the Earth's ley lines, and today the natural rhythms of the Earth are being altered with EMF. Just like our human bodies are being bombarded with EMF, so too is the Earth's body. The transhuman agenda is everywhere, silently altering the human vessel and the Earth.

Can you meditate yourself out of EMF? Can you escape it? In theory, yes. Every time you take time to raise your vibrational consciousness, in small, or large ways, you step out of, and above, the lower vibrational frequencies that beleaguer our minds and bodies. The problem is that the air is tainted with chemtrails, the water with chemicals, the food (especially in the United States) is not even biologically manufactured to nourish us, and we are glued to cell phones which alter our brain chemistry. Every few minutes we are programmed to check our phones, and if we don't, the stress hormone, cortisol, has been shown to release in most humans who use cell phones regularly. How many of us have the luxury of sitting in a cave and meditating ten hours a day? And, how many would choose to do that, if they even could? None? One? Two?

Are we choosing the transhuman path, because deep down inside, we want to become "god-like" once again, and it offers what appears to be the simpler route to our goal? I suspect that might be true. Technology gives us back a sense of power, a power most of us long to repossess. It puts the power of god in our hands, and once again reinforces the idea that God lives outside of us, instead of within us.

No one will assist you to ascend, but you. You must do the work if you want to "get off this planet, and off the wheel of reincarnation." No ET savior is going to be able to do it for you, and if they tell you they will, don't trust them. The old saying, "If you see the Buddha in the road, kill him," means just that. The true Buddha nature lives within the self, not in the illusionary being walking on the road beside you.

Part Two

What Can We Do?

CHAPTER NINE

What Can We Do?

Many people reading this book live and work with others who consider ideas of Starseeds, and alternate realities, and Extradimensional Beings, as "off limits," at best, and "whacko," at worst. I hear all the time how lonely you feel because you don't have people to talk to, or others who understand some of these ideas. It can be difficult to find an individual with an open mind, or to find someone willing to debate these ideas without prejudice or fear. (People rarely admit to fear, even if it is a common reason to block a conversation about ETs or EDs.)

Research by people as pre-eminent as John E. Mack (Harvard University) or David M Jacobs (Temple University) does little to open the minds of those who desire to keep them shut around the topic of Extraterrestrial alien abductions. Most Americans are lost in a belief system that advocates the idea that your government works on your behalf, even today. Although other countries have lived through dictatorships in recent history, Americans are often like little children, believing that the boogey man always resides somewhere else, and that your parents will keep you safe.

If you pair the need to cling to the "old definitions," of God and Country, with the fear of appearing crazy, you get a population who doesn't question authority, or get out of their own way. We seem to be moving into the direction of greater duality, and an unwillingness to enter into a friendly exchange of ideas with another person. Defensiveness appears to be on the rise, making it even more difficult to find a soul mate to discuss some "off the matrix," ideas with. So, what do we do?

1. Keep our mouths shut, and our heads down?
2. Introduce uncomfortable ideas to people, and ask about their viewpoint, even if we risk alienating them?
3. Keep smoothing over everyone's furrowed ego, to keep the peace?
4. Ignore the issues that are creating environmental, political, and socio-economic problems, and figure that God, Angels, ETs and other "higher beings" will take care of them for us?
5. Point out chemtrails and HAARP clouds to others?
6. Speak about our experiences even if they include alien encounters?
7. Figure out how to be true to ourselves, and still be kind and gentle with others we disagree with?
8. Divorce a spouse that doesn't understand us, or that we don't understand?
9. Ignore the news, or do we listen to it?
10. Hide, or should we become activists?
11. Think global, and act local?
12. Give up?
13. Soldier on?

These questions, and more, are the types of questions that Starseeds and Lightworkers ask me almost every day. It appears that so much "truth and fiction," have been mixed up, that the human race is responding in the only way they can. They are "hunkering down," in their own private bunkers of ideology and ideas.

One of the exercises I often pose to my workshop students, and private clients, is this: *Pretend that you are the Shaman of a tribe of Native Americans, and after meditating with Great Spirit you see the future. In the future you see your tribe being slaughtered by the white* man, and your world being eradicated. Do you tell the tribe, so they can fight, even if you know they will lose in the end? Do you keep your mouth shut and tell no one, assuming that ignorance will be more blissful until the end? This is an actual dilemma that many of us have faced in a previous lifetime.

These are the types of questions a Starseed is often faced with, even today...as visionaries and seers we often "know things," that others do not. How we deal with this knowledge tells us a lot about ourselves. Warriors want the opportunity to defend themselves and their people, and they would feel angry if denied that right. However, many others want to keep their head in the sand, and believe that everything is okay, even when it isn't. As the Shaman you must decide whether to impart information or keep it to yourself. It can feel like a huge responsibility at times.

If you know that there are factors endangering the survival of the human race, do you tell others, or remain silent? We have been hearing "false" end of the world scenarios for thousands of years, and we are still here. But, we have also never had this technology at our fingertips; this ET technology changes the playing field. It changed it in Atlantis, and it changes it today. This technology changes everything.

What I have noticed is that very rarely will someone take a middle position anymore. I think our unconscious (and sometimes conscious) fear creates this tougher dualistic stance. If, however, you look closer at a person's position, you will more than likely find truth within even the craziest ideas. Those who choose the role of telling humanity the fact that they believe we are charting a dangerous future path for the human race, risk ridicule. A perfect example of this is the manner in which mainstream newscasters take turns attacking author and lecturer, David Icke, and calling him insane, because he believes in Reptilians and UFOs, and the idea that human beings are not free on this planet. I'm not asking to believe everything he, or anyone else says, or to "like" him; but I think it is worthwhile to look at how someone so "off the matrix," like David

Icke, is treated, and to take a deeper look into his ideas. David Icke was the first person in the Western world to bring such "out of the box ideas" to many of us. He is tough, and he can be very irritating, but, I am willing to listen and decide for myself.

However, the newscasters admonish him, and instead of saying things like, "David Icke, who has purported for many years that Reptilians and Reptilian/human hybrids exist on the planet Earth, as many others do," the newscasters state, "Would you pay $100 to sit for twelve hours and hear a man speak about lizards who control the planet and the fact that the moon is a space station? Well, hundreds of people are doing just that."

Then the newscasters laugh their nasty little laugh and denigrate both David Icke and anyone who wants to hear what he has to say. So, I ask, if this guy is so flipping crazy, and not worth listening to, why did you spend so much time on the television denigrating him, and making nasty snickers about him? If David Icke has nothing to say, then why are you allowing him to say it, through you, on a prime news station, only to laugh at him? Does anyone ask that question? Probably not. Instead they laugh right along with the news anchors, and the ideas that David Icke purports are now relegated to the insane. It appears that we are not allowed to have an intelligent discussion about the pros and cons of someone who is so clearly "off the matrix."

When I watched David's 10-plus hour presentation in New York City a few years ago, I felt him to be a much more "likable" person, than he often appears on YouTube. But, as he says, "I'm not trying to win a popularity contest." What he is really attempting to do, I believe, is to get people off the lower-matrix of control, and to get them to question the nature of reality, as it has been taught to them.

What about the astronaut, Edgar Mitchell, who claimed that aliens exist? Do the news anchors balance the ideas purported by David Icke with Edgar Mitchell, or John E. Mack, or David M. Jacobs? No, they snigger and make sure all discussions are ended. We must ask ourselves, why? Why bring it up at all, if just to snigger?

More than likely it is because we are not supposed to think outside the box. Pure and simple. We are to think like everyone else and laugh at anyone who has a different thought.

This is also what's behind the mixing up of "fake news," and "real news." It leaves the human race powerless and confused. We have been lied to about so many things that we lack the ability to know truth; and even care. We have gotten to the point that we assume right out of the gate, we are being told half-truths and lies. A world cannot function built on lies and confusion, any more than a family, or a workplace, can.

It appears we are being manipulated to look in directions that are ultimately of no benefit to humanity. It appears that the divide and conquer agenda is in full swing, and we are stepping into it quite willingly.

Where, then, does it leave someone who thinks outside the box? Can you be free of the "lower matrix" and still be sociable, kind, open-hearted, open-minded, and yet uncompromising when necessary? I think the answer is, "Yes," but it takes work, and sometimes you will have to be involved in conflict

Revolution is usually bloody, and causalities are inevitable. If someone is taking away your rights, it has been shown that you will have to fight to hold on to your right to be free from your oppressor. Why? Because the oppressor doesn't want to give up the power they have over you. As we all know, while you are looking at someone as *your* oppressor, often they are staring right back at you and they believe you are *their* oppressor!

I am not advocating violence. Quite the opposite, as violence feeds the lower-matrix consciousness and keeps us in anger. However, you will suffer casualties as you live Truth, and do not attach to the lower matrix or the Black Goo. It is possible that you will suffer loss of friendships, and a feeling, at first, that you lost the world you once knew.

When I began to question the nature of reality, I took things off my platform, one by one, until I knew I had to stop or lose my footing. I then began to rebuild an authentic platform to stand upon. Creating a more authentic platform for yourself, requires you let some things go; and pick up other things. Being honest with the world about who you are is scary, but, essential to ascension. You can't be your ascended self and simultaneously live a lie about who you are.

Most of us Starseed/angel types are peaceniks. We are tired of war, and tired of the ancient wars. We are tired of fighting, and killing, and being reincarnated over and over into a world that we don't feel fits our soul matrix. We want peace, but it seems impossible to achieve. People ask me, "What can we do?"

I would, of course, be remiss if I said there was *One Thing*, that everyone could and should do. Each person reading this brings their own beliefs, talents, and limitations to the question "What can I do?" Some of you are born with the burning desire to become political activists, and you will find many past lives when you "fought the good fight" for freedom.

Others of you are healers, and you feel that your gifts are in healing others. Perhaps you are a fairy spirit out of Lyra and resonate with plant medicine, or crystals. Perhaps you are Arcturian, or Pleiadean, and find that your skills come directly from energies that flow from your fingertips, and eyes.

Perhaps you are gifted with wisdom, and a fierceness that allows you to speak, and to hell with what others think of you.

Each of you are expressing your gifts and giving them to the world in your own way. That's good. That's what makes you feel good, and others benefit from your gifts. But, there are pitfalls to being a Starseed and I have seen many of them expressed through my over twenty years of doing this work.

<u>Some common pitfalls include</u>:

1. Ego attachment to your gift and arrogance. I have heard stories of many gifted healers who proclaim that they are the only one who _____ (fill in the blank.) For example, I'm the only one who can wield the sword of Michael on Earth, or I'm the only one who has a direct line to Merlin's gifts.

   These ego attachments are just that, and the work that comes from someone who expresses those ideas ends up empowering *them*, and not their students or clients. We can all access Jesus Christ, we can all access God Consciousness, we all have access to Mother Mary and Mary Magdalene, or Krishna. We can all access Archangel Michael, or Ariel, or Gabriel or Raphael. We may resonate more clearly with one of these Great Beings, but we are not their sole representative on the Earth. If someone has raised their vibrational frequency enough to commune with a great archangel, then have at it…GOOD! There is no exclusivity except vibrational, and anyone can raise their vibration if they choose to. We would all be better off if we keep Jesus' words foremost in our minds and pass them to our friends, and students: "This and more, shall ye do."

2. Fear. I've spoken about this briefly, but the most common fear among Starseeds and Lightworkers comes from past lives of torture and imprisonment for their gifts. Almost all the female Starseeds I know recall lives of either: burning at stake, being stoned to death, being thrown in a dungeon, or alienation from their community. Sometimes a Starseed will have experienced all four of them and others to boot. Being attacked, killed, imprisoned or alienated in other lives often brings us to fear in this one and because of this we can be hesitant to express our talents. If a Starseed is surrounded by abusive people, or even non-believers, they will often repress their power and talent.

When the power or talent is repressed, it leads to disease and imbalance in the body.

3. Unwillingness to confront the inner shadow. This is extremely dangerous in any Starseed, especially those who heal others, or proclaim to be capable of leading others to an ascended state of consciousness. If the shadow self is repressed, instead of understood and healed, then the students, patients, and clients will be forced to carry the Starseed's shadow. Unconsciously the Starseed will project their own shadow upon others and cause emotional turmoil in those around them. This often happens without the Starseed even realizing what they have done.

4. We are naïve, and easily swayed by people and cults who promise us heaven. This is often because we are not aware of dark people and dark energies in ourselves and others. I have removed Black Goo, and other entities from clients who picked them up from sessions with other healers. If you don't understand how the dark side works, or you can't recognize the dark energies, you can easily be "tricked" by them.

5. Being lured by fame, recognition, sex, or money into situations that later turn out to dis-empower the Starseed...or in worst cases imprison them in contracts that require them to "sell their soul," or dumb down the talents and truths they want to share with the world. Giving in to the lure for power; this is what got many a dark wizard in Atlantis to turn to the dark side. There is a reason that Jesus said, "No," when the Devil told him he could make him "king of the world."

6. Being unwilling to give up dark contracts made in other lives for fear of retribution, or a loss of talents or power. This is far more common than most Starseeds realize, because it is rarely

admitted to. The few people I know who admit they are getting their power from the dark side have fit into these two categories:

a.) They don't want to release themselves from the implant that is giving them the power they crave. (Psychics often fall into this trap and category.) For example, I coached a psychic who was getting her power from the dark side. I agreed to show her how the "light works." She was powerful, and able to achieve many things, such as helping trapped souls to move beyond the lower astral, however, she got no recognition or adulation for doing that quietly, and with love in her heart. When she told me that she would rather do things as she had been doing, I said, "our time is done then."

b.) They are terrified of retribution from the dark side.

7. Taking jobs "beyond your pay grade." This goes along with the ego, but, it is important to speak about this. Know what you can and can't do, for example, if someone needs an exorcism and you are unsure what to do, or have fear, don't say, yes. We all have our gifts, and weaknesses, but make sure you don't go into areas that you are unsure of. Don't make promises to do things that you can't really do. I question whether someone can really protect you against chemtrails, HAARP, EMF or other such things just because you pay them a monthly fee.

8. Don't let fear stop you from speaking up. You have the right to be who you are (even if it doesn't always feel that way.) Be respectful and generous but find a balance between being a doormat and a bully, when it comes to asserting your point of view.

9. Recognize that you have a physical body that needs attention. This is a pitfall that many an ethereal Lightworker falls into. We want to be all spirit, and at times we wish our physical

body would just "go away," or at least stop bothering us. Years ago, I was at a Lightworker's Conference and one of the main speakers stated that he ate all "junk food." He said he liked it, and so he ate it. He believed that his vibration would overcome the sugary cereals, candy, and cheese puffs, that he consumed. It wasn't that he *occasionally* ate these things as we all do, he *almost exclusively* ate these things. Many of the attendees were shocked, because they were of the mind that they needed fresh fruit and vegetables to sustain their bodies, and some were very strict about their eating methods in order to "raise their vibration." Although I fully understood the teacher's point of view that the vibration of the food could be raised by his vibration, I felt that the ignoring of the physical vessel's needs is a trap we all fall into. Perhaps if we did nothing but float in an ecstatic vibration of love all day the constant consumption of non-nutritional food would not be an issue, but if you are racing around, riding subways, fending off chemtrails, and dealing with personal stress and deadlines, your body needs proper fuel to keep its balance. We are more than spirit while housed in the physical vessel, so I think we could all stand to pay a little more attention to the vessel. On the other hand, let's not get neurotic about it either, it is a temporary shell that we *rent*...we do not *own* our bodies, we rent them. Your body is a temporary vehicle for your spirit; honor it while you have it, but don't clutch to it like it's all you are.

10. Don't assume you are protected against all difficulty just because you are a spiritual person, or a Lightworker. If that was true then all the Tibetan monks wouldn't have been slaughtered by the Chinese, or the Cathars by the Pope, to site just two examples. You are in the world, and the world contains a collective consciousness that contributes to its reality. Everyone thinks that it is impossible that their children and grandchildren will be hurt, even while they watch news stories about other

people's children being hurt. You are a part of a very large world, and your karma is always with you. You can be walking in Central Park listening to an audiobook of *The Secret*, and the next thing you know, a bicycle slams into you. (Something like this happened to someone I know, and she could laugh about it.) There are many "realities playing out," and you can't control all of them.

11. We are one family, and as Atlantis proved to all of us...we rise and fall together.

12. Don't preach to others who are not ready or interested in your ideas. Be quiet and humble about your gifts and allow others to seek you out. If you do this you can be certain the "right people" will find you and your work, and the "wrong people" won't plague you.

These are some of the most common pitfalls that I've witnessed over the years. But, what are our strengths?

Our Strengths:

1. We are often able to see a big multi-dimensional picture and release ourselves from the third-dimensional box.
2. We have an intuitive connection to spirit and we are comfortable sitting in silence with spirit as company.
3. We are fierce. Especially the dragons. We can use this to protect the weak and helpless.
4. We are kind, and most of us try to listen to our "heart centers" and act accordingly.
5. We are strong in faith. Our connection to spirit gives us a powerful faith in a Higher Power.
6. We are willing to consider other points of view as equal to our own.

7. We are willing to challenge conventional mores and beliefs and stir things up when needed.

8. We have an intuitive understanding that something "isn't right" about much of what we have been taught, or told, and are willing to become Seekers of truth.

9. We are willing to look beneath the surface, and see in synchronicity, and experience, teachings sent to us by our Higher Self, or our Spiritual Guides. We look deeply to gather the gifts, blessings, and lessons, that hide within the events of our lives. We understand that when we look with a "spiritual mind," we see life as a series of profound lessons.

10. We realize that technology is not "the answer to everything," and that simplicity is often preferable to technology.

11. We feel connected to nature as "mother." We understand that she is to be revered, and not raped.

12. We have gifts that go beyond the ordinary: we can heal, and help others, in ways that are truly unconventional.

13. When we avoid the pitfalls, and express our strengths, we are a force to be reckoned with. Our collective energies are stirring up the world in ways that feel chaotic, but we have the ability to see the "bigger picture," and understand what's happening beyond our noses.

To be effective we must be willing to call out injustice, when necessary. It is not about protecting our little patch of turf that we own. It's about stepping outside of our human ego and asking ourselves, "What is going on here?"

If you are afraid to read Wesley Strieber's famous book, *Communion,* then read it. If you are afraid to know about your life at the end of Atlantis, then dive in. If you are afraid to speak up to your spouse, then do it. If you hide your opinions from others, then express them. If you talk too harshly to others and act like your opinions need to be forced upon others, then back off. Mix it up, in your own little world. Try something different in your behavior. Admit that the old behavior probably isn't working too well anymore. See a movie you are afraid to see. Visit the Holocaust Museum now that you know you died in the holocaust in your last lifetime. Kick yourself off the couch, even if it is only the couch in your emotional/mental body and do something out of your comfort zone. If you feel that you can't do that, then ask yourself why? Why are you afraid?

One of the most powerful experiences that spiritual seekers report having is a week-long silent meditation retreat. Silence is the most powerful thing we can give ourselves. If you are afraid of silence, then seek silence as a means to get to know yourself, and clear some of the deeper blocks.

We have to start with the self, before we reach out to others. But, working with the self is a type of boot camp. Once you get through boot camp you have to step onto the battlefield. As a soldier, if you step onto the battlefield unprepared you will be injured or killed. That is the same for a Starseed/Lightworker.

It is part of the human condition to want instant gratification, and Americans are being trained to expect it. This is counterproductive to a deep spiritual cleansing, and that is why so many go to silent retreats to reconnect with themselves. Drugs offer a type of altered consciousness, and an escape, that so many appear to need these days. I am *not* a fan of Ayahuasca, especially when it is used randomly and is *not* being taken in the presence of a trained shaman. Using a drug, such as LSD, or Ayahuasca, to get off the third-dimensional matrix, will work, but the fourth-dimensional realm is filled with dark energies that can attach to the user. Knowing how to navigate the fourth dimension seems necessary before ingesting a drug designed to take you there.

Many spiritual seekers have told me that they feel this life is about taking the gifts, and the higher consciousness, into the world, not sitting in a cave and meditating. I agree. I believe that we are meant to be activists in this life and give our gifts to the world. But, we must be prepared.

If you are a musician, you must study music, and if you are a dancer, you must study dance, before you step onto the stage. It's the same with our gifts. Our studies prepare us, as they prepared Jesus during the "Lost Years." Jesus was an activist. Gandhi was an activist. We must act in the world, and yet, we must be properly prepared before we do so.

I have written in my other books that at times I felt I was "thrown into the deep end of the pool." Yet, I swam, and while I was swimming I learned a great deal. Sometimes you will feel that you have been thrown into the deep end of the pool, as well, but if you know how to learn from the experiences your Higher Self is giving you, you will emerge stronger and much better prepared to tackle the opposition and release your gifts into the world.

Fun is a product of the lower matrix, and often we feel no heart attachment to the "fun" we are having. Joy, on the other hand, occurs when you connect your empathetic, compassionate, heart-center to your work. This is why artists and healers continue to "work" into old age and can't imagine retiring. Because their work brings them joy; and if they didn't work they would lose the heart connection to their Divine Self.

CHAPTER TEN

Protecting Yourself And Releasing Yourself From Fear

One thing we **can do** is protect ourselves. As I mentioned in a previous chapter, the Family of Light concentrates their efforts on protection of self, and protection of sacred knowledge. We avoid attacking, whenever possible, because we know to do so will bring us into a karmic agreement that ties us into darker dimensions. Once we attack, we are hooked by karmic cords into the person we attack, and as Lightworkers, we are attempting to *free ourselves* from these karmic cords, not create more. This does not mean that we won't attack when drawn into a dangerous situation which requires self-defense, but as any authentic martial arts teacher tells his/her students, "avoid engagement whenever possible."

As a result, it is important to understand how to deflect psychic attacks and repel dark energies, without being drawn into the battle. Because Family of Light has a natural aversion to darkness they feel safer if they are naïve. What I hear most is, "If I think about these things, they will come after me." Obviously, I have numerous examples that contradict that idea. My answer to those who think their innocence keeps them safe is: "Would you send your four-year-old into a dark alley in the middle of the night? No. You teach your child that there are bad people in the world, and how to avoid them. You don't believe that teaching a child to avoid bad situations, or protect themselves by dialing 911 in an emergency, brings the bad things to them. So, why do you think that learning fourth-dimensional safety makes you less safe? It is illogical and speaks to the deep-seated fear you have about the dark side."

When men come to me to learn how to protect themselves against psychic attack, they often say, "I was taught how to fight, how to shoot a gun, and how to be tough in the world, but this is something completely different. How do I fight an unseen energy?"

Although I have written about my own experiences with this in other books, it is important that you understand something of my personal experiences in this regard, so I am going to repeat some of the information here. First, and foremost, I knew nothing of any of this when I first encountered dark energy. I was naïve, as many of you are, and didn't understand how prevalent the use of psychic attack was among the Family of Dark. I also wore very thick rose-colored glasses, and like many of you, I didn't want to know about the dark side. I also didn't understand how many people are harboring these dark energies: friends, family members and work associates. People we interact with on a daily or weekly basis can be "possessed" by these energies, and most of us either ignore it, make excuses for it, or live in a co-dependent denial, and agree (unconsciously) to participate in the game these people are playing.

It doesn't have to be as complex as the example of the False Ashtar. It can be as commonplace as drug and alcohol addiction," rageaholism," and emotional abuse. Someone without any of those apparent issues (at least on the surface) can also harbor a dark nature that presents occasionally; like a shapeshifter. Most of us have witnessed a person who appears to be "possessed," and felt the dark energy suddenly emerge from them as they "twist into a different person."

Of course, the most commonsense thing to say (at least on the third dimension) is, avoid them. Avoid the people who drain you emotionally and psychically. Don't put up with emotional or physical abuse. That advice is logical. How to leave an abusive relationship, I will leave to traditional therapists. What I am talking about is insidious attacks from dark witches, wizards, and the fourth dimensional Archon energies that possess humanity, as well as targeted attacks such as the ones that hit us from EMF and satellites. This type of technology was first used by the Russians in the 1970s against Americans occupying the American Embassy in Moscow. Dubbed "Project Woodpecker," or "Russian Woodpecker," by the Americans, this attack was an early experiment to understand how these (unseen) energies of low frequency could target a person's brainwaves and drive them into depression and anxiety. When the entire embassy began to exhibit depression, anxiety and mood swings, the American military realized that this was a weapon. Recently, it appears this type of attack was repeated in Cuba, on the American diplomats there! HAARP, and the EMF affect the brains of all of us; but, nowadays the technology is sophisticated beyond 99% of the world's population's understanding.

That doesn't mean we aren't affected by these energies; in fact, I learned of HAARP in this manner. Years ago, I asked my guides why I was "feeling earthquakes" in my body. They said, it's not the earthquakes, its HAARP. Google it. (Yes, they tell me to google things.) So, I did, and it began my research into this phenomenon. Shielding yourself against targeted weapons attacks is difficult, but not impossible. And, you don't have to wear a tin-foil hat to do it. I will discuss this shortly.

My first real entanglement with dark energy was when an entity, which was hiding out in a client's body, emerged and attacked me full on. It was very much like out of a horror movie, the phone lines went down, hats and scarves flew out of the coat closet upstairs (witnessed by my husband), and the entity threatened me. My client's voice became dark and disturbed and it threatened to "get me." It also said, "You don't know who God is," when I tried to encourage it to go to God, and the Light. That began many, many years of psychic attacks, as this entity stirred up other dark energies. I have been psychically attacked (off and on) for twenty years; and I have learned a thing or two about it, since that time. I try to share my knowledge, born of experience, with whomever will listen. As I said before, not too many people want to listen. At least, not until they are attacked. Then they contact me. I think forearmed is forewarned.

Some of the Symptoms of Psychic Attack

1. Anxiety. This will be targeted to your specific fear. Knowing where your fears reside helps you to recognize this type of repeated attack: Money/poverty, abandonment, death, disease, being alone and unsupported, considered crazy, unlovable, locked-up, falsely accused, freedom taken away in any form. Recognize your deepest unresolved issues and know that these are getting directly targeted by Archon energy. Learn to recognize the fear when it arises and understand it to be a targeted attack. To counter the attack, reach upward. Remember your connection to God and All that Is. Develop a mantra and meditation method that instantly lifts your vibration. Use it. (If you can raise your vibration during an attack, you win, they lose.)

2. Feeling shaky. Your body, and/or bed vibrating.

3. Ringing in the ears…usually only one ear. A sudden intense ringing, is *not a positive download. If you doubt this simply ask, "Angels, if this ringing in my ear is not for the highest good, please stop it now."* Ask three times. It will disappear unless it is a physical condition requiring medical attention. It always does for me.

4. Depression, especially following a betrayal by friend or loved one. This causes the energy field (aura) to weaken and it can't repel negative energy as effectively. A hole or tear around the heart, or solar plexus, or any chakra point, weakens the body

and makes it easier for the Archon energy to attack. This often leads to disease in the physical body, such as cancer.

5. Talking yourself down; or believing that your "mission" is worthless and you might as well give up. Feeling all together hopeless.
6. Anger and meanness in you. Snapping at people, betraying people, and wanting to do them harm. Becoming overly critical and judgmental.
7. Losing time for long intervals. Feeling really spacey and ungrounded.
8. Finding yourself "re-hooked" into the third-dimensional matrix. By this I mean, convincing yourself to "go back to sleep" and live a "normal" life. Telling yourself that these ideas are all ridiculous. Looking for a third-dimensional explanation for a very multi-dimensional experience.
9. Waking up with unexplained scratches on your body; or even scratches on an object.

These are all examples of attacks. They might all symbolize a slightly different attack; but they are all designed to put you back asleep, or make you give up. In extreme cases, they are designed to frighten or even kill you

If you aren't honest with yourself, it is clear to see, that you can easily fall "back asleep."

Learning to protect yourself requires vigilance and the willingness to work at it without getting discouraged. You are becoming a multi-dimensional warrior, and that isn't going to be accomplished overnight. More and more people are becoming possessed with dark energy, and one of the reasons is because more and more people are casting spells "against" other people, and "playing around," with demonic entities. If you feel that someone is targeting you, don't ignore your intuition. First call in the troops: Jesus, Archangel Michael (and the other archangels), your spirit guides whomever they are. If Sitting Bull makes you feel stronger, and he is a guide, use him. Then follow these suggestions:

1. Shield yourself. Because these attacks are happening in the unseen dimension, you must fight them with unseen energy. Entering and exiting the physical body, as you fall asleep and wake up, you are very vulnerable. Intend protection prior to falling asleep every night. (Many angelic humans report coming back into their body at 4 a.m. after a very busy night, working in the astral realms!) If you are being attacked a brick wall won't stop these psychic attacks, but an "astral" wall will. Begin with light (usually white) as an egg around the body, and then create a mirrored and reflective surface facing outward on the outside of the wall. The light raises your vibration and creates a vibrational wall. The mirrored surface reflects energy back to the sender. Call in Spirit Guides for protection both before you fall asleep and during the day.

2. Repeat, "Whatever you have sent to me, I send it back to thee." Say it three times, whenever necessary. These first two work well with psychic attacks sent to you by other people. This works with the idea of "instant karma," and resides within universal law. Do not add anything to the energy; just return what is sent. The lack of emotional attachment on your part, coupled with the instant karma (allowed by universal law) makes this a clean return

3. Use the name Jesus Christ to deflect demonic attacks, and Gray aliens. There are theories as to why invoking his name over and over works…but it does. Perhaps because you believe it does, or perhaps because the energy is pure White-Christed-Light. Whatever the reason, it works. I was attacked by demonic energy one night in my sleep, and I sat up in bed, and opened my heart, and allowed the light of Jesus Christ to flow through my heart chakra as a river toward the demonic energy. WHOOSH! Instantly gone, and I slept soundly. Although I have never had a Gray alien visitation (that I remember) I have heard many times

that when people invoke the name Jesus Christ they scatter. After all, he was an exorcist while alive on the Earth. (Another reason why we should be too.)

4. One night, while on vacation in a B&B with my husband, I noticed the bed was shaking very, very slightly. It wasn't noticeable when we were awake watching TV, or talking, but, as soon as we settled in for the night I noticed a tremor. At first, I thought it might be a ghost in the old house that the B&B occupied. But, that didn't feel quite right, because I felt the energy coming from up above and targeting us directly downward. It was driving me crazy. I called on my guide, Merlin, and I started to work with protection. I built a shield out of thick metal (with my mind) and placed in the sky above us, and I imagined the targeted beams hitting the shield. I immediately felt better; but, shortly it started again. I rebuilt the shield thicker, and stayed with it, using my consciousness to keep it in place. After about three attempts I was able to hold it there and the shaking stopped completely. I fell asleep soundly. I believe this was coming from "outer space;" either from a satellite, or perhaps a Reptilian space ship, or perhaps some type of frequency attack mentioned previously. In any case, it worked. With practice, the shields can be built and maintained without too much effort.

5. Using Merlin's Spin Technique to clear negative energy. Merlin works with the vortex energy, and you can access him and his technique by merely asking for assistance.

Step One: Begin by saying: "Merlin please assist me to clear my home from negative energy.

Step Two: Imagine a vortex (tornado) energy beginning at the basement of your home and spinning up and out through the roof of your house. As it spins imagine the dark, dense energy being lifted by this vortex. Send the energy into the heaven realm to be reprogrammed. Use your intuition to determine how long it needs to spin.

Step Three: Reverse the spin.

Step Four: Stop Spin.

Step Five: Ask the archangels to reprogram the energy in your home. Dear Archangel Michael (and any others you work with) please infuse my home with your energy of: Love, Peace, Grace, Prosperity (and anything else you need.)

Step Six: Seal the home with the energy of White Light. Place an egg-shaped cocoon of white light around your house and ask the archangels to seal it. Imagine a mirror surface on the outside of the white light to reflect negative energy away from your home. Then put up any additional shields you feel are necessary.

6. Djinn is the word for spirits, used throughout the Middle Eastern world. In the West, we adapted the word Djinn and created a word, genie. It is said that Djinn can be either good or bad; but, I suggest that you never trust a Djinn. Even the so-called good ones appear to be offering a "devil's bargain." In the Middle East, Muslim spiritual prayers are often used to repel them. It is also said that if you hold onto iron or have iron jewelry they seem to be repelled by it. The use of iron is used throughout mythology; for example, it is said that the surrounding of a grave yard with an iron fence, keeps out the evil spirits. I don't have a clue as to why. Because the word Djinn isn't Western, we rarely use it, and don't know much about them. I believe they are what we call poltergeist, or demons. They are said to be created from the "smokeless flame of fire." I have a theory, but it's mine alone, so understand that you won't find others purporting this. There are people who believe that the Sahara Desert was created by a

nuclear war between Extraterrestrials on this planet. I believe that the Djinn are the souls of those exterminated in that war; and they are caught in a "between dimension." The old stories of genies (jinn) in the bottle comes from this idea. I believe that opening the "bottle" is like opening a portal, and occasionally they pop into our dimension. Sometimes they help the person who releases them, and sometimes they harm the person. In any case, they are to be avoided. Don't make any Djinn deals; the old "three wishes," from fairy tales might not be a fairy tale, after all. I have heard stories of people who have made deals with the Djinn; they are exactly what we would call a "demon deal," for fame and wealth.

This is what I use to release Djinn from your body: grasp onto iron (like a fireplace poker) and hold it until your body and hand feels very hot. Do not release the grasp, even though you will want to. Call on Jesus and Archangel Michael (other religions use other deities) to assist you to release the energy from your body, and when you feel the energy begin to lift, imagine either one of them (or whatever deity you use) catching the "smoke-like entity" in the bottle. When your body cools down while holding the iron, you will know it has cleared. That's what I do, and it works for me.

7. Astral parasites can attach to your body in the fourth dimensional realms and drain you of your life essence, or Chi. Recently, that happened to me because of time spent with a very intense energetic vampire. The next day I felt drained and exhausted. Before I went to sleep I did a prayer and asked my guides, including Merlin and the angels, to please remove the energetic parasites. I imagined them being plucked off my body, like ticks, and then a powerful vacuum-like vortex sucked them from the top of my head. I then brought in light and sealed my fields. Try this: Dear Archangel Michael, Archangel Raphael, Merlin, and all angelic frequencies of healing, please assist me. Please

bring down the vortex of Light and remove all astral parasites from my field. Imagine them being plucked off your body and sucked up in an enormous vacuum above your head. When this feels complete say, "Thank you." Then reprogram your energetic field by saying, "Archangel Raphael, and beings of Light, please infuse my body with your golden rays of Light." When that feels complete say, "Please seal and protect my body, mind and spirit."

8. To protect yourself from cursed jewelry, or other items given to you, you must first be willing to realize that the item is cursed. Don't feel guilty about your doubts. If someone gives you something, and it doesn't feel right, get rid of it. The Family of Dark often uses jewelry and other items, such as crystals, to hold negative vibrations. They will fill the item with a curse and it acts upon the intended. If you have doubts about an item, chances are there is a reason. Throw it out. Don't purchase a crystal that doesn't feel right. Trust that brilliant intuition that you live by.

9. Take salt and detox baths. Using running water over your body, while you imagine the dark energy flowing off of you, is a very effective way to cleanse. I will imagine the water as a violet color to transmute negativity. Using salt draws out the stagnant energy but won't protect you against a demonic energy.

10. Burn sage and other incense. Burn these with your windows and doors open to clear stagnate energy. Won't repel demons, but will clear out stagnant energy, and reprogram it.

11. Crystals and stones. Selenite is perfect to use as a protective stone. Build a selenite shield with crystals placed around your property. With your mind create a shield of light that is connected to these stones. Black tourmaline is good to ground you but won't work against demonic energy. If you are drawn to a particular stone, use it. Again, trust your intuition.

12. Orgonite. It doesn't block EMF, but, can alter the vibrational field in your home or around your body. Many people claim that it helps them to sleep better. It is available for purchase

online. Shuganite is also a stone used to protect against EMF and negative energy.

13. Aromatherapy. Again, useful to raise the vibration of a person. If you do Reiki healing, for example, aromatherapy is quite a wonderful added touch to calm and redirect the energy from negative to positive.

14. Energy work: If you have tried all of these and they don't seem to help, seek out the assistance of a trusted healer. Trusted is the most important word here; if someone isn't resonating with you, then they are not the right person for you. Doesn't mean they aren't good, or real, just means they might not be right for you. A healer who is comfortable talking about demonic energy, is who you want to seek out, if that's what you think is bothering you, or possessing you. Don't go to someone frightened by what might be possessing you, because they will put you in a deeper state of fear. Fear is low vibrational. Releasing fear of demons is high vibrational. It takes a very high vibration to work safely with this sort of stuff; that's why Jesus is the expert.

15. If you believe yourself to be a targeted individual, used in military experiments, or alien targeting, that you cannot handle, here are websites that offer help:

www.quwave.com/defender
http://targetedindividualsua.weebly.com/
https://www.meetup.com/TI-Awareness/messages/board...
http://www.targeted-individuals.com/counter-measur...

Please note: Scratches on your body, or objects, come from demonic realms. Scars on the body come from alien implants. The scratches are much more random, and the scars appear as small surgical scars.

The methods listed above are some of the ones used to assist me (and others) against psychic attacks. But, I must mention a deeper healing technique, that I believe is necessary for many dark attacks to stop. If you are chronically depressed or blocked, you must understand the reason the attacks are happening.

This means that you must dig through your Akashic records to find the karmic lesson, or the past life karma, or the "soul purpose" for the attacks. Many Starseeds have past lives in covens, Egyptian temples, Atlantean wizard caves etc…You have made enemies throughout your past lives. Sometimes it can be jealousy. Many a witch, wizard, priest or priestess who had some real power was hated by the "want-to-be's" that surrounded them. Everyone wanted to be the "top dog," and if you had the seat, you made enemies.

Another example of a past life scenario you could be working with is that you had tremendous power and you misused it against others. If so, you made enemies.

Another past life scenario could be that you were tortured until you relented and gave yourself to the dark side. Now you want to be free, but, they don't want to let you go.

There are many past life scenarios that create karma. Forgiveness of yourself for your transgressions, and asking forgiveness from those you harmed, is a big part of the healing. Don't play the victim. Take charge of your own healing, and protection.

It is very important that you don't allow others to make you feel bad about being psychically attacked. If you encounter someone who says something like: "If you had enough love in you, then you wouldn't be experiencing this," a good retort is: "If Buddha was attacked by the demon Mara, and Jesus wrestled with the Devil, and demons, it stands to reason that we will have encounters as well. Those beings certainly held great love."

In fact, it can be true that the more Light you hold, the more you will attract the dark energies. Angelic beings and Starseeds are targeted precisely because they are energetically powerful, and they hold much Light. Because of this, they are a threat to the Family of Dark.

The Family of Dark sees others in this way:

1. You are a member of the clan today and you do their bidding willingly.
2. You are a member of the clan because of contracts made in other lives, and they use you, with or without your knowledge, …to attack others. If you try to get free of them they attack you.
3. You are considered an enemy because you align with the Family of Light. Then they target you to try and weaken you.
4. You are useless to them, except as a food source. You do not challenge their hold on the planet in any real way, so they leave you alone until they need to feed.

If you are being attacked, it is _not_ a sign of your "badness," but of your willingness to move through darkness into mastery, just as Buddha and Jesus had to. Jesus and Buddha can serve as your teachers, not to worship them, but to emulate their examples. Be proud of your courage. Once you have overcome your fear of the darkness, you can shine your Light without fear. This is, after all what we are striving to accomplish, is it not? Your bravery will inspire others to take the journey through darkness into true Light.

And finally:

This was given to me directly from God Consciousness while I was wrestling with intense fear, after discovering my past life in the concentration camp at Dachau.

Remember how you have lain on your back in the sun? You lift your hand to block the sun's rays and find your tiny hand can cover the sun and create darkness on your face. The sun is so large, and yet you think your hand has blocked it from your face. Fear is like your hand. Fear blocks the light of God and makes you think it isn't reaching you. But, the fear is so infinitesimal compared to the power of God, that it could never block it. It merely makes you think that you have; just as your hand thinks it has blocked the entire sun. Stand back a little, and you will see your hand in its true proportion.

CHAPTER ELEVEN

Living The Truth Of You

The reason we do any spiritual work is to reclaim the Truth of our nature. We are seeking answers to such questions as: Who am I? Why am I here? What is my soul purpose? How can I live a more fulfilled life? What our ego says is, "I want to be happy." What our Higher Self says is, "I want to know myself in Truth." Whether we live a happy life, or an unhappy one, our physical body will die, and our soul will live, because it is immortal. Everywhere we go, there we are. Past lives, future lives, present life, life in other dimensions, it doesn't matter. The one thing that is consistent is you; your soul may claim another body, or take off to another dimension, but, you can't escape yourself.

Doesn't it stand to reason that we should find peace within? This third dimension is both a prison, and a classroom. It's a prison when we become a victim to the horrors. But it's a classroom when we ask ourselves, "What is the gift, blessing and lesson of my experience?" When you feel squeezed from all sides...go up! Go up, and from that higher perspective, look down upon your situation. This gives you much greater clarity.

You are in this dimension, born to your parents, married to your partner, parenting your children, or involved with certain people for a reason. Nothing is as random as it appears. Once you dig deep within, you will find that all the pieces of the puzzle fit perfectly. Learn to mine the soul's wisdom; your soul's wisdom. Dig to heal. Dig to know. Dig to integrate. Do not be afraid of yourself. You can't escape yourself, so you might as well make peace with you. Mastery is the end game. Not over others, but over the self. Not through control, but through liberation.

Young souls try to control as a means to mastery: control the body, control the mind, control what happens to you. Old souls understand that the mastery already exists, perfection is all around you, but it is your job to recognize it. Even in the difficulty. Move into your Old Soul age with the deeper wisdom of the soul. Do not deny that darkness is half of the Tao. But, also recognize that within the dark is a dot of light, and within the light is a dot of dark. Balance and wisdom through your inner Tao, is the soul's purpose in any dimension.

Enjoy the dig. Nothing that you have done, or that others have done to you, is unforgiveable. Remember, "They know not what they do." That phrase has applied to you at times. Are you deserving of forgiveness when you acted out of ignorance? If you are, then so too, are others. Of course, that does not mean you must be a door mat to the ignorance of others. It does not give others the right to harm you. But, as you recognize that you deserve to be free of harmful relationships, you begin to free yourself. More often than not, we are our own worst enemy.

Freedom comes when you free the mind, and the body. Connect to the Highest Aspect of You. It will always bring you to a right place. The ego may abhor the answer the Higher Aspect gives; but the Higher Aspect knows that whatever path it chooses serves you well. Don't walk through life with blinders on, pretending that things are other than they really are. Seek the Truth. It's painful to see clearly, but it is the only way real change occurs. Lies do not serve our soul's purpose. Stop running and start digging. Dig to move forward. Dig to ascend. Dig for freedom. You'll be glad you did.

CPSIA information can be obtained
at www.ICGtesting.com
Printed in the USA
BVHW032057301220
596688BV00003B/230